AN ALETHEA IN HEART PUBLICATION

LECTURE NOTES ON THEOLOGY

REPUBLISHED BY THE EDITOR

RICHARD M. FRIEDRICH

ALETHEA IN HEART

8071 Main St.

Fenwick, MI 48834

(989) 637-4179

TruthInHeart.com

2005

CHARLES G. FINNEY PROJECT.
BY ALETHEA IN HEART MINISTRIES.
THE LIFE AND WORKS OF CHARLES G. FINNEY.

Volume

1. Lectures on Revivals of Religion, 1835, 1868.

2. Narrative of Revivals, or The Revival Memoirs of Charles G. Finney.

3. Skeletons of a Course of Theological Lectures, 1840.

4. *American* Lectures on Systematic Theology, 1846. Vol. I.

5. *American* Lectures on Systematic Theology, 1847. Vol. II.

6. Lectures on Systematic Theology, *Final* 1851 London edition. Vol. I.

7. Lectures on Systematic Theology, *Final* 1851 London edition. Vol. II.

8. The Character, Claims and Practical Workings of Freemasonry, 1869.

9-16. The Published Sermon Collection.

17. The Published Letters.

18. Life Work and Memories of C. G. Finney by his Associates, Students, and Friends.

19. Theological and Philosophical Lecture Notes.

20. Miscellaneous Letters, Sermon Outlines, Articles, and a Detailed Subject and Scriptural Index of the Complete Works.

Reproduction of the complete works in hard and soft covers is to be available in print individually and in a complete series. These works are available on CD, and will eventually have full searching capabilities. An audio recording of these works is also planed.

Work books and multimedia helps are to be created to assist in the private or classroom study of these volumes. A presentation of the influence of Finney upon the church and world is to be given through the *American Reformation Project.*

LECTURE NOTES ON THEOLOGY;

OR,

INTRODUCTORY LECTURES FOR THE STUDY OF THEOLOGY.

BY

REV. CHARLES G. FINNEY,

PROFESSOR OF THEOLOGY AT OBERLIN COLLEGE.

EDITED BY

RICHARD M. FRIEDRICH

———

2005

Finney, Charles G., 1792-1875.
Lecture Notes on Theology; Or, Introductory Lectures for the Study of
Theology.

Publication of Charles G. Finney's Theology Lecture Notes,
Fenwick, MI.

Library of Congress Control Number: 2005920601

ISBN 1-932370-10-2 Hardcover

Third Alethea In Heart edition published in 2005. Transcribed from a
microfilm copy of *The Finney Papers* at Oberlin College Archives.

To order more copies visit our web site: TruthInHeart.com
ALETHEA IN HEART
8071 Main St.
Fenwick, MI 48834

(989) 637-4179

PREFACE BY THE EDITOR.

THE following "Lectures on Theology" were transcribed from handwritten teaching notes of Charles G. Finney. The notes were first copied and typed by Gordon Olson while visiting Oberlin College in 1953. According to Mr. Olson they were found in the fourth floor historical locked section without a file number under teaching notes.

Concerning these lectures Mr. Olson wrote:

". . . I also found an Introductory Course, Lectures I to XII, 266 pages, handwritten, which I estimated from references made to be about 1860. Its content suggests what Finney intended to be part of Volume I of his projected four volume series on Systematic Theology, only II and III of which were published and were reprinted somewhat revised in a single London volume in 1851 and abridged in 1876 for the common U.S. Printing."[1]

Since 1953, the handwritten lecture notes, along with most of the Finney papers at Oberlin College, have been put on eleven reels of microfilm. These are available through the Oberlin College Archives. The contents of this volume, along with all the other theological and philosophical lecture notes, and all other books and sermons published by Finney, will appear in a new series of volumes in 2005, titled: *The Life and Works of Charles G. Finney.*

---

[1] One correction needs to be made to Olson's statement. Finney never issued, or gave evidence of intending to issue, an abridged edition of his Systematic Theology. The 1876 abridged edition of his Systematic Theology was the work of James H. Fairchild. All publications of Finney's Systematic Theology since 1876, except Alethea In Heart publications, have been derived from the Fairchild edition. The 1876 edition cannot properly be called an abridgment of Finney's Theology when Finney stated in the 1851 edition that the volume needed to be read entirely to understand it properly. This was one of the many statements removed by Fairchild. In reducing the text about forty percent, Fairchild went far beyond removing what *he* considered needless repetition, he also removed most references to persons, and many sections and chapters which he disagreed with theologically. He did not merely shorten it but also changed the main purposes for the book.

The lecture notes in this volume will also be published in volume XIX of that series, and will be titled: *Theological and Philosophical Lecture Notes*. The other lecture notes by Finney will be added to that volume.

I began transcribing these lecture notes in 1997. Finney's handwriting was very difficult to read in certain places and so there are occasional uncertain phrases, words, and paragraph numbering in this volume. The numbering of the chapters was also difficult to decide. On page 80 below, we have a proper chapter without having been numbered. The letters VI*b* have thus been given to it in order to fit with the other chapters. The complete volume first appeared on Alethea In Heart web sites in 1998, where a large library exists of the works of Charles G. Finney, Asa Mahan, and other historical and contemporary authors.

While transcribing I was so pleased with the beginning lectures that the name of the publishing ministry was changed to a key theme and phrase found on pages 28 and 29 below. The website was named *Truth In Heart* (truthinheart.com), while the actual name of the ministry is *Alethea In Heart* (alethea is the Greek word for truth). While the same lectures have continued to inspire many other persons since they first appeared, they also partly inspired the recent inception of a school modeled after the recommendations given. The School of Realistic Theology and Moral Government Theology (rpmgt.org), founded in 2004, will recommend the twenty volumes in the series titled: *The Life and Works of Charles G. Finney*, to all it students.[2]

As the question is frequently asked, In which *order* should Finney's books be read? the following suggestion is given. When I first began to study Finney, it was not long before I started studying his 1851 edition of *Systematic Theology*. I was not far into that volume before I read the following statements (in the Preface and chapter I):

"Let no one despair in commencing the book, nor stumble at the definitions, thinking that he can never understand so abstruse a subject. Remember that what follows is an expansion and an

---

[2] A similar twenty volume series, *The Life and Works of Asa Mahan*, will also be recommended among many others.

explanation by way of application, *of what you find so condensed in the first pages of the book.*[3] My brother, sister, friend—read, study, think, and read again. You were made to think. It will do you good to think; to develope your powers by study. God designed that religion should require thought, intense thought, and should thoroughly develope our powers of thought. The Bible itself is written in a style so condensed as to require much intense study. Many know nothing of the Bible or of religion, because they will not think and study. I do not pretend to so explain theology as to dispense with the labour of thinking. I have no ability and no wish to do so. . . .

"*Theology is so related to psychology, that the successful study of the former without a knowledge of the latter, is impossible.* Every theological system, and every theological opinion, assumes something as true in psychology. Theology is, to a great extent, the science of mind in its relations to moral law. God is a mind or spirit: all moral agents are in his image. Theology is the doctrine of God, comprehending his existence, attributes, relations, character, works, word, government providential and moral, and, of course, it must embrace the facts of human nature, and the science of moral agency. *All theologians do and must assume the truth of some system of psychology and mental philosophy, and those who exclaim most loudly against metaphysics, no less than others.* . . .

"I must assume that you possess some knowledge of psychology, and of mental philosophy, and leave to your convenience a more thorough and extended examination of the subject but hinted at in this lecture."

I was not familiar with psychology and did find the *Systematic Theology* difficult to grasp. This difficulty, along with the above words quoted, led me to seek out such works on psychology. This led to my discovery of the curriculum of the early Oberlin institution where Finney taught theology for 40 years, and to Asa Mahan (1799-1889), its first president and teacher of mental philosophy. Mahan authored eight volumes and many more papers on psychology and related subjects, as well as many others on different subjects. All Mahan's books are listed at the end of this volume. From around 1835 to 1850 many of Finney's theology students had also studied under Mahan's instruction in mental

---

[3] Emphasis added to all paragraphs. This is chapter I and deals with psychology: *Various classes of truths, and how the mind attains to a knowledge of them.*

philosophy for several years. Both men admittedly shared nearly identical views in theology and philosophy. It is fair to say that one who is familiar with even a few of those books would understand every word and concept mentioned in the opening chapter of Finney's *Systematic Theology*. And as Finney states, once that is understood, the rest follows relatively easily.

Another statement in Finney's *Systematic Theology* suggests that the volume before you may be part of what was intended as the first volume of his *Systematic Theology*: "Should the entire course [of Systematic Theology] ever appear before the public, one volume will precede, and another succeed the present one." The contents of *Lecture Notes on Theology,* though not as detailed as Mahan's books, give much more detail than the above mentioned first chapter in Finney's *Systematic Theology*. While it is obvious that more subjects would need to be added to this volume in order to make it the *preceding* volume, it is also clear that some of it would have been included. Finney would probably have added much of the same material found in his student A. M. Hills' Systematic theology.[4]

To understand and appreciate Finney's and Mahan's theology, methods, and success as evangelists, philosophers, and reformers, I recommend the following order of books: *Lectures on Revivals of Religion,* and *Narrative of Revivals*, by Finney, together with *Autobiography,* and *Out of Darkness Into Light,* and *Doctrine of the Will,* by Mahan; followed by *Lecture Notes on Theology*, by Finney, together with *Mental Philosophy* and *Intellectual Philosophy*, by Mahan; followed by *The Science of Logic*, by Mahan, with *Skeletons of a Course of Theological Lectures*, by Finney; followed by Finney's *Systematic Theology*, with Mahan's *Moral Philosophy;* Finally, *A Critical History of Philosophy,* and *Natural Theology*, by Mahan. The many volumes of sermons and holiness topics could be read along side all of the above mentioned works.

Richard M. Friedrich, *January* 2005.

---

[4] Aaron M. Hills' *Fundamental Christian Theology.* Hills wrote Finney's biography and thought Finney was the greatest preacher he had ever seen.

CONTENTS.

LECTURE I.

INTRODUCTORY.

I. *I will define the study upon which we are about to enter.*
II. *Notice some requisite personal qualifications for this study.*
III. *Some advantages to be derived from the study of Systematic Theology.*
IV. *Some things to be avoided.*
V. *Remarks.*

I. DEFINE THE STUDY UPON WHICH WE ARE ABOUT TO ENTER.

1. THEOLOGY is the science of God and of divine things. It teaches the existence, natural and moral attributes, laws, government, and whatever may be known of God, and of our relations, duties, and responsibilities to him and to the universe. In its most comprehensive sense it embraces all knowledge.

2. It may be, and generally is, divided into natural and revealed theology. This distinction does not imply that natural theology is not revealed, but that it is not revealed by inspiration. Natural theology is that which derives its evidence from the works of God, or from nature, as it is often but erroneously expressed. Revealed theology is that which derives its doctrines and evidence from the Bible.

3. Theology is again subdivided into didactic, polemic, and pastoral. Didactic is the systematic statement of theological doctrines with their evidences, both of natural and revealed religion. Polemic is controversial, and consists in the defense of the disputed doctrines of theology. Pastoral relates to the relations, duties, and responsibilities of pastors. It teaches the just application of the principles of the government of God, to the pastoral relation of a pastor to his people and of the people to their pastor; of his responsibility to them and to God in the instruction he gives them, and their duties to him and to God in respect to the manner in which they receive his instruction as an ambassador of God.

LECTURE II.

II. SOME OF THE REQUISITE PERSONAL QUALIFICATIONS FOR THIS STUDY.

1. We do not naturally understand the language of one with whose state of mind we have no sympathy. A selfish being will hardly understand the language of a benevolent one, but would naturally interpret his language as intended to express what he himself would mean by such language.

There is scarcely any of the language of true benevolence which is not very naturally misunderstood by a selfish mind. Therefore it is indispensable to a just interpretation of the works and words of God that we should be in sympathy with his state of mind. And it is quite natural for persons in the same state of mind, devoted to the same end and inclining to purpose that end by the same means, to understand each other's language. They naturally express themselves alike and use very much the same forms of expression, whether literal, metaphysical, or figurative, to express their ideas. Hence the first and indispensable qualification for the study of theology is sympathy with God, devoted to the same end to which he is devoted, and a heart set upon promoting it by means of holiness.

2. True candor and uprightness of mind, a likeness to God in this respect, is an indispensable qualification for the successful pursuit of this study. An unfair mind can never understand theology. In this state of mind one cannot know God. It is so utterly out of adjustment with God's state of mind as naturally and inevitably to misapprehend him. But a mind that is upright and candid, willing to do and consequently to know the truth of God as it is, will come to this study prepared to enter into it, to obey the truth, to be taught of God, and will therefore easily apprehend all that is intelligible to minds of our finite capacity.

3. An earnest desire to know God that we may honor and obey him, that we may commune with him and be like him, that we may

12

rightly represent him to others and win them to sympathy with him, is essential to a successful study of theology. If this desire be strong it will make us diligent students, it will naturally lead to the use of all the appropriate means of obtaining this knowledge, it will beget an earnest struggle after all that may be known of God, and a mind in this state will naturally acquire theological truth with great facility.

4. A right state of mind in regard to those around us is indispensable to the study of theology. A state of mind that is grieved and offended with their sins, yet having at the same time such intense love and compassion for them as to beget the most earnest desire to rescue them from their sins, to save their souls and adjust them in the will of God.

This state of mind in regard to them will lead us to study about God that we may instruct and enlighten them, that we may reprove their sins and win them to Christ. Without this abhorrence of their sins and love for their souls, we cannot understand God's abhorrence of, and love and compassion for them. To understand what God proposes respecting them and their sins, we must be of his mind.

5. A willingness to make any personal sacrifice to glorify God and save the souls of men is an important qualification for the study of theology. If we make our own ease and comfort practically superior to the cause of God and the worth of souls, our faith must be very weak, and our hearts cannot be in such a state as to appreciate the great things of theology. We need to be in a state in which we count not our lives to be dear unto us if called to lay them down for God, and to sympathize with the apostle when he said, "I count all things but loss for the excellency of the knowledge of Christ Jesus my Lord." I would not advise any young man to study theology with the design of preaching the gospel, or with the expectation of really understanding it, unless he is prepared in heart to make any personal sacrifice in favor of the cause of God.

6. Another qualification of great importance is a sense of our ignorance, the natural darkness of our minds, and dependence upon divine teaching. We need to understand in the outset that spiritual

things need to be spiritually revealed to us. Sin has greatly darkened our minds, and although without special divine illumination we know enough through reason and conscience to bring us under condemnation for disobedience, yet without the supernatural illumination of the Holy Spirit we shall never so understand or know God as to win our hearts to him, or to enable us to win the hearts of others.

It is not enough that we should read the Bible and understand it historically as we would other matters of history. It is not enough that we should be able to state catechetically or didactically its doctrines. We need a spiritual apprehension of them; we need to be taught inwardly as really as the inspired writers; and as a condition of understanding theology in any influential sense, we need divine inspiration. I do not mean that we need to be taught truths that are not declared in the Word or published in the works of God, but that we need that these things should be shown to us inwardly and spiritually—that the works of God may be spiritually apprehended and the Word of God spiritually interpreted and applied. Or, as I said before, we need to be inspired by the same Spirit with which the writers themselves were inspired, to have them shown inwardly to us as they were to them.

7. Another condition of successful study of theology is a willingness to practice as fast as we learn. If we do not yield our minds up to practice the truth we shall soon fail to understand it. The Spirit will be grieved, we shall fall into confusion and darkness, and nothing can give us a clear apprehension of the truth if we persist in refusing to obey it.

8. A fixed purpose to know and to do the whole truth is another condition of the successful pursuit of this study. If there are some points on which we are committed and opinionated, if we have some theory to maintain, some preconceived opinion or prejudice to indulge, we shall almost certainly be deceived. I have sometimes met with young men who came to the study of theology, assuming that on certain points they were settled. It would be seen that a want of candor pervaded their whole mind and course of study. But I have yet to see the first instance in which such a mind has made thorough progress in theological study. There is that want of

candor that fills the mind with darkness, rendering it impossible to obtain the true knowledge of God and of divine things.

9. A state of mind that so deeply appreciates the value and infinite importance of divine truth, that it will not be diverted and practically lay an undue stress upon other things and upon the knowledge of other truths. A young man who comes to the study of theology needs to have a mind absorbed with the surpassing greatness and value of his theme. If he can willing turn aside and be diverted by pleasure or business, by gossip or light reading, if he is disposed to attend to a multitude of other things at the same time, he can never thoroughly comprehend the great questions of theology. He must truly and practically value them above all price. A young man who is in a state of mind to spend much time in light reading, in keeping himself informed of all the newspaper gossip of the day, who can lightly make journeys of pleasure and turn aside from the great inquiry after God, who fills his mind and hands with trifling subjects, is in no state of mind to be taught of God.

10. Another important qualification for this study is such humility as shall make you willing to expose your ignorance. In commencing this study it is to be assumed by you and by others that you are not informed, that you are not a theologian, but that you need teaching. You take the attitude of students. Of course, your need of teaching is presupposed. Be not then afraid of exposing your ignorance; do not assume to know what you do not know; do not suppose that you may be expected to know beforehand the subjects that are to be given you for study; come out freely, ask questions, and give yourselves up to study, assuming that you have everything to learn upon the subject.

11. The love of study, and the love of this study in particular, is an indispensable condition to your understanding theology. If this study is a task to you, you had better let it alone. If you do not love God well enough to have an intense desire to know all that can be known about him you are in no state of mind to study theology. You need to be so interested in him as to hunger and thirst intensely for more and more knowledge of him. If this be not your stated of mind, if you are disposed to go no farther than the rules of

the seminary require, if there is not that within you that prompts you to study from love to God, and of the knowledge of God, you will never make theologians. If you can lightly come in without having studied you lesson, can suffer some trifling thing to divert your mind and cause your to fail in recitation, you are in no state of mind to pursue a study like this. On the contrary you need to be in the state of mind expressed in the second chapter of Proverbs, "My son if thou wilt receive my words, and hide my commandments with thee; so that thou incline thine ear to wisdom, and apply thine heart to understanding; yea, if thou criest after knowledge, and liftest up thy voice for understanding; if thou seekest her as silver and searchest for her as for hid treasures; then shalt thou understand the fear of the Lord and find the knowledge of God. For the Lord giveth wisdom; out of his mouth cometh knowledge and understanding. He layeth up sound wisdom for the righteous; he is a buckler to them that walk uprightly. He keepeth the paths of judgment, and preserveth the way of his saints. Then shalt thou understand righteousness, and judgment, and equity; yea, every good path" (Prov. 2:1-9).

12. A sound education is another important condition of understanding theology. By sound education I do not mean that it is indispensable that you understand the original languages in which the Scriptures are written, though this is important and of great value when those languages can be thoroughly known as to enable the student to criticize and thoroughly comprehend the original. Yet without this critical knowledge you may obtain a good theological education. There are now so many helps to an understanding of the original Scriptures, so many criticizing and marginal readings, so many commentaries and helps to interpretation so far as the theology and literature of the Bible is concerned, that great classical learning is not indispensable. If you have time and opportunity you will surely avail yourselves of the original languages if you truly love the Bible. But if you have no such time or opportunity, you may still so well understand your Bible as to be able to give sound instruction to the multitudes that may wait upon your ministry.

But by sound education is intended so much knowledge of mental, natural, and moral philosophy as will place you in a position to understand the laws and government of God, to appreciate in some measure his works; so much knowledge of history, of geography, and of learning in general that your hearers shall perceive that you are an intelligent man; so that when you speak of government, they shall see that you understand something of the science of its different departments and functions, that you do not confound in your illustrations the judgment of the court with the verdict of the jury, the summing up of evidence with the pleadings that make up the issues. You need to understand something of the laws of evidence to be able to define what evidence is, what kinds of evidence are essential to prove certain truths, understand so much of psychology as to distinguish between the rational and understanding conceptions, to know what truths are first truths, what truths are merely self-evident, what truths need proof, and when they are proven. In short, to come to the study of theology you need so much previous education that you may understand the grammatical construction of language, the force and meaning of words, how to state a proposition, how to state a syllogism, how to frame and how to appreciate an argument. In a word, you need to be generally intelligent and instructed in the learning to be obtained in schools, or from books. It is of great importance that what learning you have should be sound; that your views in mental philosophy should be sound; that you should not come to this study committed to the doctrine of the necessity of the will's actions, ignoring the great truths, the admission and knowledge of which are essential to an understanding of the principle terms to be used in the pursuit of this study.

13. Industrious habits are of the last importance. Mental indolence will be a thorough preventative of your ever being theologians. Your state of mind must lead you to be industrious, and render it natural for you to fill up your time and to lay yourself out in securing information upon this subject. An indolent ministry can never be an instructive ministry; and indolent student will not be taught of the Spirit of God; an indolent spirit may expect to remain in darkness.

14. Patience and perseverance in investigation are essential. Many of the questions to be examined require to be persistently investigated. We do not arrive at the mastery of them at once. They involve difficulties; they are questions deep and high, and of difficult comprehension to minds in our circumstances. They were designed of God to create a necessity of earnest effort, for patient and industrious investigation. We need it for our own development and discipline; and the development we obtain from patient and persevering investigation is often as valuable to us as the truth which at last we obtain. We gain intellectual vigor, and moral vigor, by exercise. God does not condescend to give us the truth without our study; but he aids and stimulates our efforts, meaning to give us truth only as we reach for it as for hid treasures. By this means we grow intellectually and spiritually.

In teaching theology, it is no part of my design merely to lecture to you, and help you to truth without your own efforts. This would do you little good, nay, it might greatly injure you. I would merely help you to study, help you when you endeavor to help yourselves; suggest to stimulate and guide your efforts rather than dispense with them. I have no sympathy with, or confidence in, that mode of theological instruction that merely reads lectures to young men. They may as well find their theology in books—and better—and remain at home and study. When you come here to study, we design to give you the question to be investigated, and as far as possible to throw you upon your own resources, upon your reading and reflection and study to find out the truth; to make you lead off and give us your views, and then to make such suggestions as to stimulate and guide your investigations to a right result, not lecturing you at all, until you have surveyed the subject and as far as possible settled your own convictions. Then after suggestion and helping you to study for yourselves, we sum up and try to state the whole question, and if possible throw additional light upon it. Thus we endeavor to make you theologians by aiding your efforts, instead of dispensing with them. We do not mean that you should merely hear and remember, but that you should investigate and make up your minds whether right or wrong; that you should have the full value of all that we can say to guide you, said in the proper place and suggested in a manner that shall give the fullest scope to your own investigations and lay as much of the burden of finding out these truths upon you as is consistent with your coming to a thorough knowledge of them. It is for your sakes that we do this. To have you come here and listen to our lectures, take notes, and go away and live upon our thoughts instead of thinking for your-selves—why this will be your ruin!

You need to make yourselves acquainted with the laws of evidence so as to understand upon whom the burden of proof lies in the settlement of all these questions, that you may not assume that which needs to be proved, nor take the burden of proof when the onus (or burden of proof) truly lies upon your antagonist. You need also to be able to give correct definitions, and to define your terms with perspicuity, and have so much knowledge and good sense as to state your propositions clearly, and then proceed to prove what you have stated, and not to state one proposition and then prove another, nor rest your cause till you have made out your case.

15. You need a correct knowledge of the laws of Biblical inter-pretation. Without this knowledge you will misunderstand your Bible, and mislead your hearers, unless in fact they are more able to teach you than you are to teach them. Many of the multitude of opinions which claim to be supported by the Bible would vanish from the world if men agreed in respect to the correct rules of Biblical interpretation.

16. Lastly, it is of great importance that you understand the limits of human research and investigation. If you forget that you are finite, if you suppose yourselves able to grapple with and comprehend all truth, you will probably fall into the disbelief of all truth. If you insist that you will not believe what you cannot comprehend, if you stand upon the proposition that your line can be stretched out and measure infinity and eternity, that you can sit in judgment when [sic.] God and the high policy of his government, and bring all these great questions within the mold of your own understanding and your own logic, you will find yourself baffled, confounded, and unable to proceed with any comfort in your investigations. Know therefore in the outset that there are

limits to all human investigation and comprehension; that we can affirm that many things are without being able to state how and why they are, or even to conceive how they can be possible.

III. SOME OF THE ADVANTAGES TO BE DERIVED FROM THE STUDY OF SYSTEMATIC THEOLOGY.

1. A constantly increasing sense of our own ignorance. Before we commence this study we are not aware of the vast field before us, and how little we know of what is to be known. The more we survey the field the more it amplifies and extends on every side. The more we attempt to solve its problems the more we are astonished at the extent of our natural ignorance and darkness. As we pursue the subject we perceive that there is ample room for an eternity of study, and that our utmost attainment here can only be as the A B C of what may be known and is finally to be known of God. Nevertheless, we may satisfy ourselves on many fundamental questions, and obtain all the knowledge that is essential to our highest usefulness and happiness in the world. It is no matter of discouragement to us as we pursue this study that it is so vast and indeed illimitable, but rather a matter of encouragement that so delightful a theme is expanded to infinity, and that we shall have enough to learn to occupy our attention and powers as long as we exist. But an increasing sense of the fact that we are in the A B C of our theological knowledge, while it does not tend to discourage, does greatly tend to humble us and make us modest.

2. Another advantage to be desired from the study of systematic theology is growth in personal holiness. The study of theology is most highly calculated to produce this result.

3. It also tends to beget the habit of rapid, correct, and con-secutive thinking. To systematize our thoughts on this subject is of the greatest importance to us. God has created us in a position and places us in relations that make it indispensable for us to think closely, correctly, and consecutively, and often to review our positions, and thus in the highest degree to cultivate our intellectual powers. A thorough course of theological study will render subsequent preparations for the pulpit naturally and relatively easy and safe.

LECTURE NOTES ON THEOLOGY.

4. It tends to beget system in thinking and in communicating thought. Ministers who have not made theology a study, find it difficult to communicate thought in that systematic and logical order that is easily intelligible to any congregation. Their propositions are disconnected, often inconsistent with each other, and hence embarrassing to a congregation. But a thorough study of theology tends to rid one of unintelligible manner of stating truth.

5. The study of theology leads us to perceive the necessity of exactness in the statement of our positions, and the doctrines of Christianity. To a theologian the manner in which a preacher defines his positions and states the doctrine which he proposes to inculcate, will reveal at once his attainments as a theologian. It will be seen whether he has thought accurately, extensively, and is really acquainted with the system of doctrines peculiarly Christian.

6. The study of theology is essential to facility on the part of the preacher in proving the doctrines of Christianity.

7. This study tends to prevent those inconsistencies of statement that so often embarrass a congregation. It is not uncommon to hear preachers make statements that are seen by thinkers in the congregation to be totally inconsistent with each other. The students in his congregation can easily perceive that he is himself no student; and in the very outset they come to have little confidence in what he has to say. He does not understand himself. He has not thought enough to perceive that his various positions and statements are inconsistent with each other. A thorough study of theology is therefore of the greatest importance to the one who would attempt to state and establish and proclaim the doctrines of Christianity.

8. This study tends to a settled state of mind in regard to religious truth. When these questions are not settled by discussion and thought, and scientifically digested in the mind, we are constantly liable to be unsettled, to be thrown into perplexity and doubt in regard to them. Satan is ever busy to unsettle us, and will be sure to make those suggestions that will embarrass us, unless we so familiarize ourselves with the subject as to know what answers to make to any suggestions with which he may assail us.

9. The study of theology gives us that ability to teach without which the minister in the active duties of his calling will either

neglect study, or will be obliged to study so hard as soon to break himself down. If he is prepared to enter the ministry by having digested and systematized the truths of Christianity, he can in sermonizing apply these doctrines consistently and with an ease that will not require of him that amount of mental labor that is unendurable.

IV. SOME THINGS TO BE AVOIDED.

1. We should by all means avoid tempting God by demanding an impossible or unreasonable kind of evidence. Some students have approached this subject and determined in the beginning to take absolutely nothing for granted. They have not considered what kind of evidence is reasonable to expect; they have therefore demanded that every truth shall be demonstrated, or seen with intuitive certainty. In settling some questions, we first enquire what proof of its truth, considering the nature of the question and our circumstances, we may expect to find, what kind and degree of evidence ought to be satisfactory; and if such kind and degree of evidence is found to be within our reach, we should rest satisfied, and not tempt God by refusing to receive a truth upon a reasonable kind and degree of testimony.

2. A caviling state of mind should by all means be avoided. It is this state of mind that leads to the rejection of reasonable evidence, and in a state of probation it is not reasonable to expect that every truth which we need to receive will be established by irresistible evidence. If it be established by evidence that will convince a fair mind and produce conviction where there is candor, it is all that we have a right to expect.

To force conviction upon a moral agent in a state of probation may not be wise or even consistent with such a state. The truths of theology may plainly be expected to be revealed with such a degree of evidence that a mind in search after truth can find out all that it needs to know; but still many things will be left in such a position that a perverse mind will find itself able to resist and avoid conviction.

Many of the truths of theology, as we shall see, are first truths, truths which everybody assumes and knows to be true. Others are merely self-evident in such a sense as that their truth is readily seen when they are once stated in intelligible language. Others are truths of demonstration; others still are truths of experience; others still are truths of history. We shall find that the system is based on a solid foundation, and that at every step there is a kind and degree of evidence that ought to satisfy a rational mind, and that will satisfy an honest inquirer. Nevertheless, a caviling, perverse state of mind can resist it all; and even the first truths of reason may be and often have been denied; and the foundation thus falling away, through this denial a universal skepticism has been the result.

3. Another thing to be avoided is, in the course of our discussions the defending of erroneous positions merely for the sake of argument. It is sometimes seen that this results in the ultimate belief of all that which was at first asserted and defended with a knowledge that it was false; and merely for the sake of argument. The feelings became enlisted, pride stimulated, and in the heat of debate the judgment became warped, and ultimately the defender of error comes to believe his own lie.

4. Beware of committing yourself to an opinion. We are very liable to do this without being aware of it. There is a natural pride of consistency in many minds, that exposes them much in this direction. With some, once a thing is asserted it must be maintained; once having advanced an opinion they seem to be blind to every argument and fact that would disprove it. It is amazing to see how difficult it is to convince some minds on any subject upon which they have committed themselves to an opinion. Some young men have been here who seemed to be unable to yield an opinion. No argument or even demonstration could shake them. They seemed not to know what it meant to yield a point to which they were committed. The will has much more influence in forming our opinions than we are aware of—and in sustaining them when they are formed. The will commands the attention; it allows the attention to perceive and weigh arguments; it in a great measure controls the judgment; it selects and arranges those considerations that can support an opinion, and refuses the consideration of those that would overthrow it. Hence it is of the last importance that we should be on our guard against committing ourselves to an opinion until we have given it a thorough consideration. Especially is this true in respect to questions upon which it is plain that good and great men have differed. Some truths are too plain to admit of doubt. To them we may commit ourselves—and indeed we cannot avoid committing ourselves to them so far as opinion is concerned. But where there are two sides to a question, when there is room for

doubt and debate and argument, then this should be our motto, "Hear both sides and then judge."

5. Avoid calling in question first truths. These truths can in no way be proven, as we shall see, except by the perfection of their chronological antecedency. If we attempt to prove them by logic we shall often find it impossible. Who by logic can prove that time or space exists? Who by logic can prove that every event must have a cause? These truths cannot be proved for the reason that they are too evident to need any proof. There is nothing more simple and evident that can be laid down as premises from which they are to be deduced. They lie at the foundation of all reasoning, and are in themselves the major premises upon which we construct our syllogisms.

If these truths are called in question, if proof is demanded of them, if you attempt to prove them and fail, as you most certainly will, it may lead you into universal doubt. Suppose you call in question your own existence and demand proof of it—you cannot prove it; and if as a condition of your believing it you must be able to prove it by any logical process, you must disbelieve it and settle down into universal skepticism.

6. Avoid impatience at the ignorance or stupidity of your classmates. Regard yourselves as a band of brothers and as soldiers of Jesus Christ; consider yourselves as all interested to make the most of each other that can be made for the cause of God; be interested to develop and instruct each other that everyone may be the best soldier possible. Be not selfish, and willing to rush on and leave any one behind. Remember, if you go to the charge you need the whole strength of the army; and if you refuse to bear with patience the drill necessary to instruct and fit for service those that apprehend truth more slowly than you do, you will weaken the course which you are committed to support. Bear one another's burdens, therefore, and so fulfill the law of Christ. Endeavor with calmness and patience and perseverance to secure in every member of the class a thorough understanding of every position that is taken.

7. Avoid an ambition to excel them in study and argument. An ambitious student is detestable. I mean one who manifests a selfish

ambition; manifests a disposition to be a leader, to overshadow his class, and a pride when he thinks he rises above them and excels them as a student. Some students will even pride themselves in getting into a controversy with their teacher, and manifest a most unchristian deportment not to be instructed, but to overcome their teacher in argument. With some this seems to be a point, to get the reputation of teaching their teacher. If your teacher is in error, there is an unambiguous method of leading him to see it, and striving, not for mastery, but with a manifest searching for the truth.

You are not requested to rest satisfied without thorough investigation, and where you have not reason to be satisfied. And it is generally easy to see whether dissatisfaction is owing to the absence of sufficient evidence or to an ambition to excel in controversy.

8. Avoid therefore a disputatious spirit. This will ruin your piety, darken you mind, and make you a fool while you esteem yourself to be wise. Discussion is indispensable; and after many years experience I am fully satisfied that theological teachers and students need thorough discussion in settling the great questions of theology. Discussion should be thorough, and not cut short till reasonable time has been given for a thorough examination of all the questions to be settled. The utmost liberty should be given for the expression of opinion, the asking of questions, the statement of objections, and the array of arguments pro and con, till the positions are probed and searched to their foundations. This is our habit. This we regard as indispensable. This after many years of experience I am satisfied is the only method of settling theological truth. But it exposes to temptation in this direction, there is a danger of getting into a disputatious spirit and of becoming proud of our powers of argument and discrimination, and of getting into a state in which we cannot hear an opinion expressed, even in common conversation, without immediately calling it in question, and manifesting a disposition to battle every one with whom we come in contact. This is an unhappy and a most disgusting state of mind.

Study therefore to be modest in questioning the opinions of others. Do not consider yourselves as under an obligation to oppose every opinion with which you do not accord. Be not disputatious in spirit or manner, but always take the attitude of candor as a sincere inquirer after truth. The Socratic method of inquiring, rather than affirming, is the safest and most influential way of debating any question.

9. Avoid the use of weak and inconclusive arguments. A strong point is often rendered weak in the estimation of the hearers by attempting to support it by weak and inconclusive arguments. Let your strong points be strongly stated, established by the best arguments which the nature of the case admits; and when you have produced your strong and conclusive arguments, introduce no weak and inconclusive ones, lest you betray the very truths you intend to establish.

10. Avoid an involved method of stating your propositions. Try to state them with the utmost perspicuity, and as laconically (concisely) as possible; and leave no room for query in regard to what you mean by your main propositions.

11. Avoid stating more than you can prove. State what you mean and what you intend to prove and then stop. If you gratuitously state, or even attempt more than you are called upon to prove, it will only embarrass you and your congregation. Consider your positions, what is essential to your purpose; state that, prove that, and there rest your cause. As preachers you will need to avoid an error not infrequently fallen into by young advocates at the bar. They will sometimes call their witnesses, produce their evidence, but fall short of really proving that which in their pleadings they have affirmed. They do not legally make out their case. This they do not perceive, and therefore inform the court that they rest their case, supposing that they have now thrown the burden of reply upon their opponent. But the court and their antagonist will perceive that they have not made out their case. The opposing counsel will move the court to dismiss the case on this account—that the party has not produced legal evidence of the truth of his position. Hereupon the court will dismiss the case. Who has not often listened to sermons that amounted to precisely the same thing? When the preacher rested his cause, it was open to a motion to dismiss the case for want of sufficient proof. The congregation

might adjourn with the understanding that the question remained unsettled. Now avoid leaving your propositions until they are fully supported by evidence and argument. See that you carry the convictions of the people. Place the subject in such a light that you know that they must see that the evidence and argument are conclusive; then rest your position and make such use of them in the application as are required by the end you have in view.

V. REMARKS.

1. The study of theology demands much prayer. "No man can say that Jesus is the Lord save by the Holy Ghost," and the teaching of the Holy Spirit is promised in answer to prayer. The soul needs to be kept in an anointed state, to walk in the light of God's countenance. The study of theology demands that we should become pupils of the Holy Ghost.

2. Remember the condition on which Christ has promised to be our teacher: "Except a man forsake all that he hath," says Christ, "he cannot be my disciple." To be a disciple of Christ is to be his pupil; to be his pupil is of course to have him as our teacher; and we can have him, as he informs us, only on the condition that we renounce our selfishness. Self must be abandoned, and our whole being devoted to his service and glory; then we are in a state to be instructed by him, and then he has wise reasons for instructing us.

3. Take care that you keep your hearts with all diligence, and that your hearts keep pace with your intellectual improvement. If you do not make a self-application of the truth as fast as you learn it, if you do not obey it, it will ultimately blind instead of enlighten you. You must live up to your convictions, or the study of theology will greatly and fatally harden you. Therefore be careful that you grieve not, resist not, quench not the Holy Spirit. Study on your knees. Go to God with every position that is established, and pray him to write the truth in your heart; and rest not till it be adopted by you as your own, as a truth to influence you, to have dominion over you; and as these truths are developed in your intellect one after the other, and established, let it be settled that in the midst of them, and in conformity with them, you are to live and move and have your being.

If you do this the study of theology will make you a mellow, anointed, devoted, useful man of God; if you do it not, you will become hardened and reprobate. And of all the reprobate minds in existence, they seem to be the most hardened who have studied theology and gone through the course of theology without receiving the truth into their hearts. Every truth that lodges in the head and does not take possession of the heart, is to the student "the savor of death unto death." As you value your own souls, therefore, as you value your influence, as you value the cause of God, let it be settled that with much prayer and the utmost honesty and effort you will make every truth of theology your own, not only in the sense of mastering it with your intellect, but of embracing and obeying it in your heart.

LECTURE III.

INTRODUCTORY.
CONSCIOUSNESS AND SENSE.

STUDY implies a student; knowledge implies a knowing faculty. The study of theology implies the existence of students capable of the knowledge of God.

I. DO WE KNOW ANYTHING?

Answer, yes; we know ourselves. Should anyone say, I doubt this; I enquire, Do you know that you doubt it? Should he reply, I doubt that I doubt it; I enquire again, Do you know that you doubt that you doubt it? Should he reply, No, I do not know anything; I enquire again, Do you know that you do not know anything? Should he say, No, I only guess that I do not know anything; I enquire again, Do you know that you thus guess? Should he reply, It only seems as if I thus guess; I enquire, Do you know that so it seems? Should he reply, No, this seeming is nothing; I enquire again, Do you know that this seeming is nothing? Should he reply, No, but only so it seems; I reply, Then you are sure that so it seems; and if you are sure of this, or if you are sure that you are not sure of this, it amounts to the same thing. We know some-thing—we know ourselves; it is impossible to doubt this.

II. HOW DO WE KNOW OURSELVES?

I answer, in consciousness. That is, we are directly aware of ourselves in what we call consciousness. But what is conscious-ness? The word has been used ambiguously. Some times as the general faculty of knowledge; in this sense Sir William Hamilton often used it. Sometimes it is used as a function by which we know ourselves. Sometimes it is spoken of as self-knowledge. It is common to use the term as signifying either that particular function of the intellect by the use of which we know ourselves, or the knowledge of ourselves given by this function. More generally the term is used in this last sense, to signify self-knowledge; but often the faculty by which we obtain this knowledge is called by the same name by which we designate the knowledge itself. The connection in which the term is used will in general show the sense in which it is used. If we speak of the intuitions of consciousness, of course we speak of it as a function or faulty of self-knowledge; if we speak of self-knowledge as a consciousness, then it is plain that by consciousness we mean the knowledge of self.

I say then, IN CONSCIOUSNESS WE KNOW OURSELVES. Of this knowledge I remark:

1. That it is intuitive knowledge; that is, a knowledge obtained by a direct beholding of ourselves in the exercise of our various faculties.

2. I remark of this knowledge, or of consciousness, that it is a certain knowledge, knowledge of the highest possible kind, a knowledge that cannot be doubted. To call its validity in question is to question the validity of all knowledge, which we have seen, is nonsense.

III. WHAT DO WE KNOW OF OURSELVES IN CONSCIOUSNESS?

1. We know our existence. This is not an inference; "Cogito ergo sum," (I think, therefore I exist, Latin) is a mere sophism. If I am not directly aware of my existence, how do I know that I think; and from the consciousness of mere thought, what right have I to infer that I think, or that I exist at all. There is no premise from which this can be inferred. The mere consciousness of thought affords not the least evidence that I am the thinking substance, or that I exist. And why should I say, I think? The very language implies that I know that I am, in knowing that I think. The very conception of thinking includes the assumption that I am. In consciousness, then, I know my own existence.

2. In consciousness I know that I have three distinct faculties: The faculty of knowledge; the faculty or susceptibility of feeling; the faculty or power of willing, choosing, acting. I know in the exercise of these different faculties or susceptibilities, that I posses them. I know, for instance, that I know; and in this knowledge I know that I am and that I have a faculty of knowledge, because I am conscious of using it. I know that I feel; and in the exercise of

feeling I know that I possess and use the power or faculty of willing and choosing. This knowledge, this feeling, this willing, I know to be my own; and it is impossible for me to doubt either the exercise or the existence of the faculties thus exercised.

3. In consciousness I know all of myself that is knowable by me of myself.

4. In consciousness I know myself as distinct from that which is not myself; and in the very conception of myself as self I know that that exists which is not myself. Of this I am in some way as certain as that I exist myself. Indeed the conception of self implies the conception of not self. Self can be defined only as we discriminate between that which is self and that which is not self. I am, then, in consciousness directly aware of myself, which implies that I am also aware of that which is not myself.

Because of his peculiar definition of consciousness, Sir William Hamilton insist that this awareness of that which is not myself is strictly a consciousness. It is true that we are conscious of knowing that there is a not self; but is not this knowledge an intuition of the faculty of perception and distinct from consciousness but known in consciousness? It is sufficient to say that whether this as a knowledge of the not self, is a direct intuition of consciousness, or is an intuition of the perception faculty, which intuition is given to us in consciousness—certain it is that we have this knowledge, which we can no more doubt than we can doubt the knowledge of ourselves.

5. In consciousness we know that the intellect has various functions; some of which are: Consciousness, sense, reason, conscience, memory, imagination, etc. Of consciousness I shall say no more at present, as it has been, for our present purpose sufficiently defined. Of sense, reason, and conscience, more things need in this place to be said.

IV. WHAT IS MEANT BY SENSE?

Sense is that function of the intellect by which we directly intuit the material world, including our own bodies and all material objects. It has been common to regard sense as that function of the intellect that intuits sensation. Sensation is an impression in the sensibility made either by some material object, or by some thought or action of the mind.

Sensation is a feeling. I once received the common idea that sense perception was merely a perception of the sensation, a feeling in the sensibility; but I do not now so regard it. Philosophers who have regarded sense as merely giving sensation have found it impossible to find any valid proof of the existence of an outward cause of sensation. They have said truly, that sensation being a feeling of the mind has in it none of the qualities that we attribute to bodies, and consequently that from the sensation we cannot infer the qualities of body or the existence of those outward things which we suppose have created the sensation.

This difficulty has stumbled many philosophers, and they have admitted that there was no valid reason for believing in the existence of the material universe. But other philosophers (as Sir William Hamilton) maintain that sense does not give us sensation, but that we are directly aware of sensation in consciousness—that we are directly conscious of the feeling in the sensibility which we call sensation, and do not know it by a sense of perception. This class of philosophers maintain that by sense we directly perceive the primary qualities, at least, of material bodies.

The sensationalists object to this, that it is impossible to conceive how sense can directly perceive the qualities of external bodies. But to this it is justly replied, it is also impossible to conceive how sense could give us sensation.

We know not how it is that we are directly aware of ourselves, or how it is that we directly intuit anything in consciousness, sense, or reason. How an impression upon the sensibility should be irresistibly known to me, I cannot tell. The fact I know; the how I do not know. So it is with all our knowledge. Certain it is that we do not get the existence and qualities of external objects as an inference from sensation. We actually know that we do not thus get it—that we have the knowledge not as an inference from premises. That we do not get it logically we know just as we know our existence.

For example, in knowing the material world around me I know that I do not get at it in this way: Phenomena imply substance;

substance is as its phenomena are. Here are the phenomena; these phenomena imply substance, and this substance must be as the phenomena are; therefore such are the material substances around me. Now who is not aware in consciousness that this is not the way in which one gets a knowledge of his surroundings?

Who, for example, ever looked at an object and reasoned in that way, or could conceive himself as getting a knowledge of that object by such a process of reasoning? No, we are directly aware that we perceive it. Certain qualities of it are revealed to us irresistibly and directly. The object stands face to face with the perceptive faculty; and its primary qualities are as surely known to us as our own existence, and precisely in the same way, only through the use of another intuitive function of the intellect.

In consciousness I directly know my own existence; in consciousness I know also that I directly perceive the existence of other things. The faculty that directly perceives material objects I call sense. It would be out of place here to enter into an inquiry with regard to the particular attributes or qualities of the outward world that are given in sense. This inquiry is in place in a treatise in psychology, but it is unessential to our present course of study. For the present it is enough for us to know that by the function of sense we know with certainty the existence of the material universe.

Of this function, then, in conclusion, let me remark, first, that it is an intuitive function of the intellect, gets all knowledges by a direct beholding. From the very nature of its perceptions, its testimony is to be received as valid. Nay, it is impossible to doubt the validity of its revelations. Let philosophers deny as they will the existence of the outward world; they know it still, and give as constant evidence to themselves and everybody else that they know it as other men do.

It should here be remarked that intuitive knowledge is always irresistible knowledge, by whatever function of the intellect the intuition is given. In intuitive knowledge the object known and the knowing faculty stand face to face. Such is the nature of the objects of intuitive knowledge, and such the nature of the faculty of intuition, that standing face to face we cannot help knowing these objects. They are directly beheld, and known with irresistible certainty.

It should also here be said, that in consciousness we are aware of sense perceptions and of all that passes within us; so that with whatever function of the intellect knowledge is obtained, in consciousness we have the report of all these knowledges. The same is true of our feeling, willing, imagining, remembering, dreaming, and whatever passes within us.

LECTURE IV.

INTRODUCTORY.
REASON.

LOCKE's philosophy of human understanding logically resulted in atheism. He maintained that all knowledge is founded on, or derived from, sensation, or from sense. Now it is plain that sense can give material facts but not principles and laws. Hence, legitimately no inference whatever could be drawn from the facts of sense or sensation. It could not be inferred that there was any cause whatever of these sensations, for sensation knows nothing of cause. If no faculty of the human mind gave the idea of cause and effect, and the law of causality, all that could be known by us would simply be the material acts that occur. It would be impossible for us to refer them to any law or cause whatever. Therefore, the inquiry after cause, upon the principles of Lock's philosophy, was entirely impertinent.

The logical consequences of this theory were gradually perceived by philosophers, and those of a skeptical tendency seemed very willing to admit the soundness of his philosophy, and to triumph in its logical consequences. As was logically necessary, it finally brought forth its fruits in the atheism of David Hume and his school. Hume simply [?] upon trust the Christian philosophy of his time, and pushed it to its logical consequences. This result lead Kant, a German philosopher, to call attention to the existence and province of an *à priori* function of the intelligence, to wit, the pure reason, as this function is given in consciousness. He asserted, and philosophers now generally admit, that we are conscious of a faculty that directly intuits laws and principles, as consciousness intuits our inward experiences.

I. WHAT WE MEAN BY THE REASON, AS DISTINCT FROM THE OTHER FUNCTIONS OF THE INTELLECT.

1. I have said that it is the *à priori* function of the intellect as distinct from, and opposed to, the logical function, or the *à*

36

posteriori function of the intellect. The *à posteriori* function of the intellect gets its conclusions or knowledges from reasoning, or from induction; this, the *à priori* function, gets its knowledge from a direct beholding or intuition.

2. The pure reason gives or is concerned with ideas, as opposed to concrete existences. Reason gives ideas and their mutual relations, as opposed to the mutual relations of things and beings. The reason gives laws and principles as sense and consciousness give facts or phenomena. Reason gives certainties as opposed to hypotheses; reason gives the necessary as opposed to the contingent; reason gives the unconditional as opposed to the contingent; reason gives the infinite as opposed to the finite; reason gives the perfect as opposed to the imperfect; reason gives the ideal as opposed to the real; reason gives the axiomatic as opposed to the logical. Reason does not prove but affirms; reason does not suppose but knows; it does not deduce but postulates; it does not give the exceptional but the universal; it does not give plurality but unity; it gives truths of certain knowledge as opposed to opinion or belief.

3. Its knowledges are all universal and irresistible, as opposed to those truths that can be really doubted. In the course of study that is before you, it is of great importance that you should continually keep in mind the distinction between the rational function of the intellect and some other functions of this faculty; because, whatever is directly intuited by this faculty is to be taken as a truth of certain knowledge. By this I do not mean that the same is not true of consciousness and sense within their respective spheres; for they also are intuitive functions of the intellect. But whatever is given by this faculty is to be distinguished from whatever is given by the understanding, the judgment, the imagination, or memory. Its truths are peculiar in their kind, being self-evident, necessary, and universal, they are therefore truths of irresistible knowledge. No one of them can need to be proved, because it is a truth of direct and certain knowledge. I will now proceed to notice two classes of truth given by this function: First what are commonly denominated first truths of reason.

II. FIRST TRUTHS OF REASON HAVE THE FOLLOWING CHARACTERISTICS.

1. They are self-evident; that is, they are truths of intuition, perceived by a direct beholding of them. They need no proof because they are irresistibly seen to be true in their own light. They stand face to face with the intuitive faculty. Such is the nature of these truths, that the mind cannot help knowing them. It knows by a certain, direct, and irresistible knowledge, as when you open your eyes with your face toward the sun you cannot avoid the sensation of the sun. So the reason, in the presence of its objects, that is, of those truths adapted to its nature, cannot avoid beholding them. All the truths of the reason have this characteristic; but at present I speak of first truths as being universally self-evident.

2. Another characteristic of first truths is, they are necessary as opposed to contingent truths. The reason does not merely perceive that they are so, but that they must be so. The reason does not merely affirm that they are true, but that their opposite is impossible and absurd.

3. A third characteristic of first truths is that they are universal as opposed to the exceptional or general. That is, there are no exceptions to these truths. The reason affirms not only that they are true and that there is no exception to them, but also that there can be no exception to them—not only that they are but that they must be universally true.

4. First truths are truths of certain knowledge, as opposed to opinion, speculation, belief, or even demonstration. Truths of demonstration are affirmed by the reason to be certain, provided there is no mistake in the premises; but as mistake in the premises is in many cases possible, they are not certain the sense in which first truths are certain. These truths are not deduced from premises in which there may be mistake; but being truths of direct intuition they are truths of certain knowledge in the highest sense. We do not merely believe them, or opine them, or demonstrate them, we know them by a direct certainty.

5. First truths of reason have this characteristic, which, in fact distinguishes them from all other truths; they are truths of universal knowledge, the denial of them always and necessarily involves a

38

contradiction. That is, all beings in whom reason is developed do actually assume and practically acknowledge their truth, even though they may never have made them an object of attention, or even have been aware that such truths are known by them. They may never have been thought of in the form of a proposition, and yet they are known, assumed, and always acted upon. In specifying some of these we shall see that they have these characteristics.

III. EXAMPLES OF SOME FIRST TRUTHS OF REASON.

1. The existence of space is a first truth of reason. It is a truth known and assumed by every rational being. We find it impossible to doubt the existence of space, even if we suppose the non-existence of everything else. This is a universal knowledge, and has all the characteristics that have been specified as belonging to the first truths of reason.

2. The existence of time is also a first truth of reason. All rational beings know that time exists. Although in consciousness we find that we can conceive of the non-existence of all things in time, yet time will remain; to conceive its non-existence we find in consciousness to be impossible.

3. The truth that every effect must have a cause is a first truth of reason. I do not mean that it is a first truth of reason that there is any effect, or that there is any cause in existence; but that effect and cause imply each other, that no effect can exist without a cause, and that no cause can exist without an effect. The law, then, that every effect must have a cause is a first truth of reason, everywhere assumed.

4. That every event must be an effect, and have a cause, is a first truth of reason. An event is something that comes to pass. That whatever change occurs, or whatever comes to pass, must have had a cause is a truth that cannot be doubted. It is not a contingent but a necessary and universal truth, and one that must be universally assumed and is therefore a first truth of reason.

5. That a series of causes and effects cannot be infinite, is a first truth. Every effect is a unit. Infinity cannot be made up of parts or units.

6. That time and space are infinite, is a first truth of reason. That either time or space should have limits is inconceivable and impossible. This is and must be universally assumed.

7. Another first truth of reason is that the will of a moral agent must be free. A moral agent is a responsible agent. A responsible agent is truly an agent, an actor, a self-acting being, one who originates and directs his own activity. A moral agent is one who acts under the responsibility or moral obligation. Moral obligation, strictly, respects acts of will, choices, and volitions. Now the reason directly affirms that moral obligation to will, implies power to will in accordance with obligation, or the contrary. That a moral agent must be free—not in the Edwardian sense, able to execute his volitions, for this he may not have power to do; but free in the sense of being able to will as moral law requires him to will, or will in an opposite direction at his sovereign discretion. This ability is liberty of will. The reason directly intuits and affirms that this liberty of will is an indispensable condition of moral agency, and that this is a necessary and universal truth. It is a truth also known to, and affirmed by, all moral agents; and no being could conceive of moral obligation to will unless he assumed the ability to will.

These are only some of the first truths of reason, given as specimens. It will be seen that they consist in ideas, laws, and principles, as distinct from concrete realities or proper beings.

IV. HOW THESE TRUTHS ARE DEVELOPED IN THE REASON.

I next proceed to notice the condition upon which these truths are developed in the reason. They are necessarily known to all rational intelligences. The inquiry at present is how they came to be thus known, or the conditions upon which they are thus known.

1. The first condition upon which they are known is the existence of this function of the intellect, as distinct from the other functions of the intellect. The sense, like the reason, is an intuitive function of the intellect; and so is consciousness. But sense gives only the material; consciousness gives the facts of our existence and mental acts and states; but reason gives not these, but pure abstractions. This is the peculiarity of this function. Reason gives

the logical antecedents of sense perceptions. Sense gives the chronological antecedents of rational conceptions.

2. A second condition is a fact given, as a sense perception. Sense perceives an object possessing the qualities of extension, form, solidity, whereupon the rational idea of space is developed. This perception is the chronological antecedent, and the necessary condition of the development of the idea of body and the affirmation that space exists. The ideas of body and space must be simultaneously developed; for they cannot be thought or defined except as they are distinguished from each other, body and space. The existence of body is not affirmed by the reason; but the perception of body develops the conception of space and the affirmation that it really exists. Sense gives the existence of that which the reason calls body, without affirming anything of its actual existence. But of space it not only has the conception of what it is, but also affirms that it is. The idea being once developed, the actual existence of space is affirmed by us as a necessary truth. The idea always lies in the mind as a first truth, whether thought of or not. It is always there, assumed and acted upon by a necessity of our nature.

3. How we come by the first truth, time is. This truth may be developed either by some conscious succession in our inward states, thoughts, or feelings, or by the sense perception of the succession of outward events. The consciousness or the perception of succession develops the rational ideas of succession and time. These must be developed simultaneously, as a succession is seen by the reason to imply time, and time to imply the possibility of succession. The consciousness or the perception of succeeding events, within or without us, is the chronological antecedent of the development of these rational ideas. The ideas do not develop each other, but are developed upon the occurrence of conscious or sense perceptions.

The rational idea of succession is not an affirmation that events do exist in succession, but that succession implies time. The idea of succession is simply that of relation in time. But the rational conception of the existence of time, as a first truth of reason is not only and idea of what time is, but that it is, and must be. The rational idea of succession is not that succession is, but what succession must be, if it is.

Time, then, given as a first truth of reason, is that time is and must be whether anything else is or not. It is not that the rational conception of time is that of flux, or flow, or any movement or succession in it; but that it is a unit, duration, that in which succession exists, or may exist. The rational conception of time, then, is simply that of duration as necessarily existent, as having neither beginning nor end nor parts, but as infinite and a unity. Both space and time, as first truths, are given as absolute, that is, unconditional truths—their existence depending on no conditions. Hence, did we suppose that nothing else existed, we affirm that time and space must exist.

4. How we attain to a knowledge of the law of cause and effect as a first truth of reason. Either by the spontaneous exercise of our own causality, our consciousness or sense gives some occurrence or event, whereupon the reason instantly affirms that this event had a cause; and that this event had a cause because every event must have a cause, or must be an effect.

Locke in his philosophy could not consistently arrive at this; there being in his estimation no *à priori* faculty to affirm that an event must be an effect, and that an effect implied a cause, and that events imply causes or cause; he could not conclude that there was any necessary connection between events. Brown assumed Locke's philosophy, and hence consistently denied that there is any cause or effect in the proper sense of these terms. Cause and effect, with him, meant nothing more than precedent and subsequent events— not antecedent and consequent, but merely antecedent and subsequent. Hamilton denied all causality. This, on the principles of Locke's philosophy, is consistent. But the pure reason irresistibly intuits the law of causality. It affirms that no effect can exist without a cause, and that no cause can exist without an effect—that they mutually imply each other.

Hence the ideas of cause and effect are both rational ideas, simultaneously developed upon the perception or consciousness of an event. This perception or consciousness, let it be remembered, is the chronological antecedent of the development of both of these ideas. The law of causality is not a first truth of reason, in the sense that reason affirms that cause and effect do really exist, but in the sense that if one exists the other must, that they mutually imply each other, and that this truth is necessary and universal. In this form it is strictly a first truth of reason, universally known and practically assumed—as well by Locke, Krouse, and Hamilton, as by others.

5. That the will of a moral agent must be free I have said is also a first truth of reason. This is developed in the mind by the perception of that of which we affirm oughtness, or obligation, or duty. Something comes before the mind that demands the action of the will. Some outward act is performed, or some inward choice or volition to be put forth or declined. The moral function of the reason thereupon affirms obligation; and in affirming obligation it assumes ability to choose or act in the required direction. The assumption of the freedom of the will no doubt lies back of this, as from our earliest infancy we assume the freedom of our will in constantly asserting it and manifesting it in our actions. So also we assume that every event is an effect, and that every effect must have a cause. This we do in the exercise of our own causality, or in the actions of our wills put forth to produce effects. These assumptions are clearly made by us previous to the development of the rational conception of the freedom of the will, of cause and effect.

The first truth about which we are now inquiring, that the will of a moral agent must be free, is a rational conception added to that instinctive knowledge which from the beginning we posses, that we have a will and are able to use it at discretion. The first truth that the will of a moral agent must be free, is developed by the reason's directly beholding that which demands the will's action, and in the presence of the moral function of the reason affirms obligation. In the affirming of obligation by the moral function of the reason, the natural function of the reason affirms not merely that my will is free as a condition of the obligation, but this is a universal truth, that obligation implies liberty of will in the sense of power to act in either direction in the presence of obligation, and therefore that freedom of will is essential to moral agency, and that the will of every moral agent must in this sense be free.

V. DIVISION OF FIRST TRUTHS OF REASON.

The first truths of reason are strictly of two kinds. First, they are ideas of necessary existences, or what Cousin calls necessary ideas. The idea of a necessary existence is an idea which we necessarily conceive as having an archetype, the non-existence of which we cannot conceive possible. Such are the ideas of time and space. These we necessarily regard as having archetypes, or that which is represented by their ideas. Duration and space we necessarily conceive must exist; and in this sense we call these ideas necessary ideas, or more properly ideas of necessary existence.

The other class of first truths, that is, truths of necessary and universal knowledge, are not ideas of necessary existences, but ideas which under our circumstances we necessarily have. Such, for example, that a whole is equal to all its parts, and that all the parts of anything are equal to the whole; that every effect implies a cause and every cause an effect; that a moral agent must be a free agent; that a moral agent must have moral character; that a moral agent must be under moral law; ideas of right and wrong. These are some of the first truths which are given in reason as ideas which we necessarily have, but of which we do not necessarily affirm that they have any archetype.

VI. SECOND CLASS OF TRUTHS OF REASON.

1. It is common to speak of self-evident truths of reason. But it should be remembered that reason is an intuitive function of the intellect, and therefore that all its truths are necessarily self-evident. They are all developed by a direct beholding or intuition, by which it is intended that they are seen to be true in the light of their own evidence, and therefore are self-evident truths. The reason knows no other than self-evident truths; therefore to speak of self-evident truths of reason is not to designate any particular class of truths given by this faculty, for this is the universal characteristic of all the truths given by it.

But the second class of rational intuitions or truths, to which I call attention, are not truths of universal knowledge in the sense that they are necessarily recognized or known to, or assumed by, all rational beings whose reason is developed. But nevertheless they are truths of rational intuition; although in many cases where the reason is in some degree developed many of these truths are not already intuited or known. Such are, for example, the truths of mathematics, mathematical relations and proportions, the laws and principles of science—indeed, all the laws, principles, and postulates of all the exact sciences. These laws, axioms, postulates, and principles are all given by the reason when they are apprehended, are directly intuited as being self-evident in their own nature. Whenever they are apprehended the mind calls for no proof of them, because they are seen to be necessarily true. Although they are not truths necessarily known to all whose reason is developed, yet they have the attributes of necessity and univer-sality; that is, they are seen not only to be true, but necessarily and universally true from their own nature. Such, for example, as, "Things which are equal to the same thing are equal to each other." All the propositions of Euclid contain truths of direct intuition; that is, in these propositions the major premise is a postulate. The minor may be a fact, or it may be another postulate.

But in mathematical reasoning, as a general thing, the whole process is a rational one; because the relations are ideal or abstract relations, not the relations of things but of ideas. Hence, properly speaking, the science of mathematics is to a very great extent made up of rational intuitions. These are not first truths in the sense that they are universally known, but in the sense that they are necessary and universal truths, discovered by the direct intuitions of reason.

VII. HOW THIS SECOND CLASS OF TRUTHS IS DEVELOPED IN THE REASON

1. Not empirically. We do not, for example, and cannot prove by mere measurement that a whole is equal to all its parts; or that all the parts whatever of anything are equal to the whole. And could we in any particular case show that the whole is equal to the parts or the parts to the whole, this would not give us a universal truth. It would be illogical to conclude that because it was so in a

particular case it must be so in every case. It is the reason alone that gives this truth in the form of a universal and necessary truth. The chronological antecedent of the development of this, as a universal and necessary truth, might be the fact that we perceive in a given case that a whole is equal to all its parts, or that all its parts are equal to the whole. But it is plain that no experiment upon isolated facts or cases could logically give truths necessary and universal. These truths, then, are not given empirically in the sense that we logically infer them from any experiment. Experience may be the chronological antecedent of their development; but they are never a logical inference from experiment.

2. These truths are not obtained *à posteriori*. This of course is implied in their being truths of intuition. But some may suppose that a truth obtained by syllogistic reasoning is after all really given by intuition; and that therefore a truth obtained by a course of reasoning or *à posteriori* argument, might be said to be intuitively obtained. But whatever may be said of a truth arrived at by induction, the class of truths of which we have been speaking are not of this kind. They are not conclusions from premises, but are rather themselves postulated as premises. In other words, they are *à priori* truths given in the reason, not as conclusions from any other truth, but as postulates or axioms, universal and necessary in their own nature. They are, then, developed as *à priori* truths, principles, and laws, sustaining such a relation to the reason as not to be inferred from other truths but affirmed as first principles.

3. Again, these truths are developed by teaching—not in the sense of proving them to be true, but in the sense of stating them in such a manner and in such connections, as to render them intelligible and place them face to face with the reason. The teacher of mathematics, for example, is employed, not in proving these truths, but in so presenting them to the mind that the terms of the proposition in which they are stated are rendered intelligible, and thus they are placed before the intuitive gaze of the reason.

4. These truths are developed by study, in the sense of giving the attention of the mind to them. Not study in the sense of demonstration, but in the sense of meditation.

5. Again, these truths are developed in intellectual culture, in the sense of developing them in their necessary order. The reason seems to be capable of indefinite development; and all self-evident truths are not seen by it at once, but we learn from consciousness that there is a natural and necessary order for their development. A student of mathematics, for example, will not at once receive the statement of all the axioms that belong to that science; much less of the mathematical truths, proportions, and relations that in the course of development are seen to be self-evident. The human reason is not omniscient; it gets its truths by intuitions, but by successive steps, and rises from the recognition of the first truths of reason into the region of other necessary and universal truths, doubtless in endless progress of development.

VIII. REMARKS.

1. The truths of reason need no proof, because they cannot be doubted.

2. This last class of rational intuitions are not like first truths, truths of universal knowledge, but only truths that must be known in the order of their development, because when the conditions are fulfilled they are seen to be true in their own light and from their own nature, necessarily and universally true.

3. We should not assume that all the self-evident truths of reason are of course at present self-evident to all minds. Many may not yet have attained to that stage of development in which the statement of them would be understood, or in which they can even be conceived by the reason. A child, for example, that already has the first truths of reason, the ideas of time, space, that every effect implies a cause, etc., may nevertheless not have attained that degree of development in which it could understand the terms in which many axioms and postulates of science are stated. In all steps of intellectual development we shall find that as the reason advances, the field of self-evident truths is enlarged, the number of these truths multiplied. Innumerable truths would be self-evident to a Newton or a LaPlace, that could not so much as be conceived of by children and youth.

4. Again, we may not suppose that many truths may not be self-evident to others which are not so to us. On the one hand we

have no right to suppose that all minds, whatever their degree of development, will intuit all the truths that we intuit as necessary and universal truths; nor on the other hand make our own degree of development the limit of intuitive knowledge, and assume that what we do not know is not knowable, what we do not intuit is not a truth of intuition. The reason of this difference is not that reason in it laws, modes of activity and affirmations is not identical in all; but it is a question of development, of progress, there being no end to the progress of development. The first truths of reason are developed through the instrumentality of sense perceptions at the very dawn of reason. No one probably can remember when he had not the ideas of time, space, cause and effect, and the law of causality. But we can all remember how gradually our reason has come to the apprehension or intuition of many necessary and universal truths.

5. Again, it is important in teaching or studying for us to inquire to what category any given truth belongs. Is it a first truth? Then everybody knows it. We may well assume that those around us know it. Although they may not have thought of it, still they know and assume it; and we may safely proceed with them upon the assumption that this truth is in their minds as a certain and irresistible knowledge. But if it is not a first truth, but a truth belonging to the class which we have just considered, a necessary and universal truth but not a truth universally known, we need, if teaching, to proceed to fulfill the conditions of its development.

6. Again, we need to consider the natural place or connection in the order of development which such a truth sustains to the reason. It is a familiar fact to us all that after considering a matter well, many truths are seen by us to be self-evident, as necessary and universal truths, which at first we did not see to be so. This is a constant experience in the study of the exact sciences. By this I do not mean that these truths did not appear to us to belong to this class, to be self-evident and universal, when we really apprehend them; but that the apprehension of them required study, consideration, and the fixing the attention upon them.

With respect to truths of reason, then, it should be said, that to develop first truths of reason, objects should be presented to sense perceptions that will serve as chronological antecedents to spring them into development in the reason. Let sense perceive body, and anything be said or done that shall spring the idea of its being body, and with this idea is naturally also sprung the idea of space. So, call attention to the fact of succession in a manner that shall spring the idea of events being separated in time, and it forces into development the rational apprehension and affirmation of the existence of duration. In a modified sense of the term this may be called the proving of first truths of reason; but only in the sense that you fulfill the conditions of their development, and not in the sense that you present an argument, or logical formula, or proof, or evidence according to the common acceptation of these terms.

Of the other class of truths of reason, I would say that it often happens that they may be proved in this sense, by the *reductio ad absurdum*—that the denial of them involves a contradiction or an absurdity. Truths of reason, sense, or consciousness, can seldom be proved by any process of argument, for the reason that there is no truth more certain in the light of which they may be established or from which they may be inferred. And it is often dangerous to volunteer an attempt to prove these truths, because a failure to prove them might lead to their being called in question, when in fact the reason why they cannot be proved is because they are the major premises of syllogistic reasonings. To attempt, therefore, to prove them is to overlook their nature and their relations to the intellect, and consequently virtually to represent them as doubtful or as needing proof; whereas it should be understood that all truths of intuition, whether of consciousness, of sense, or of reason, are not only too certain to need proof, but so certain that they cannot be proved, except as I have said, by the *reductio ad absurdum*.

I make these remarks, because in the course of study upon which we are entering, it is important that we should understand what we are to prove, and what we are to take for granted as needing no proof—that when any truth lies in our course of study that is plainly a truth of intuition, its truthfulness cannot rationally be called in question.

IX. TRUTHS OF CONSCIENCE.

I have already said that conscience is a function of the reason, or is reason applied to moral objects. The truth of this is evident because conscience is plainly concerned with ideas, qualities, laws, principles, and relations—with the abstract, the necessary, the universal. I call that conscience, that upon certain conditions being fulfilled, affirms moral obligation; that postulates the great rule of moral action; that affirms the law of universal benevolence as an authoritative rule in conformity with which all moral agents ought to act. The conception or affirmation of this rule as a rule of duty, as implying and enforcing obligation, is given by the moral function of the reason.

The ideas, then, given by conscience are such as these: Moral law subjectively affirmed or imposed by the conscience, moral obligation or oughtness; the ideas of right and wrong, of moral character, vice, virtue, desert, justice, injustice; the ideas of moral attributes, qualities and relations; the idea of God as a moral governor; the idea of God's moral attributes as distinct from his natural attributes, which are given by the natural function of the reason. Reason applied to natural objects gives God as a first cause and as infinite in all his natural attributes. Conscience, or the reason applied to moral objects, gives the moral attributes of God, and his relation to his creatures, not as cause, but as governor, or as having rightful authority. The natural function of the reason gives God as naturally infinite and perfect, while the conscience gives him as morally infinite and perfect. Conscience gives the idea of virtue in its universal form as the moral quality of disinterested benevolence; and it gives all the moral qualities or attributes of disinterested benevolence as virtues. It gives the idea of justice, mercy, veracity; in short, the idea of virtue and vice in every form in which virtue and vice can exist. The quality virtue or vice, as affirmed of any action or state of mind, is given by the conscience, is perceived and affirmed by that function of the reason.

Feelings arising in the sensibility as a consequence of the intuitions of conscience are strictly no part of conscience; but only a result of its affirmations and intuitions; although in popular language we often speak, and the inspired writers appear to speak, of conscience as including these states of the sensibility. But speaking as philosophers in the light of conscience, we regard the conscience as purely an intellectual function, as belonging to the pure reason, and as strictly consisting in reason applied to moral questions.

X. HOW THE IDEAS OF CONSCIENCE ARE DEVELOPED.

It has been common for skeptics to suppose that conscience is altogether a matter of education, and that morality, or our ideas of morals, are mere prejudices, the result of education and a superstitious tendency. But is should be observed that had we not a conscience that necessarily gave us these ideas, men could never be educated in morals, or have any prejudices upon that subject. Were not the ideas of moral right and wrong irresistibly given as first moral truths, children could never be taught that anything was right or wrong, except in the physical sense of these terms. It is in vain to tell a mere animal that a thing is right or wrong. It has not the idea; consequently, if you could make it understand language, to say that this or that particular thing or act is morally right or wrong would be totally unintelligible. Not having the abstract idea of moral law, nothing can be compared with it, or brought into its light so as to be conceived of as right or wrong. The mind must have a law, and a moral law, in its intuitive conceptions or affirmations, as the condition of having any conception of moral right or wrong in the life. The rule can never be given by teaching. But the rule once in the mind, we can teach children or others what particular acts come under it as being in accordance with or opposed to it. But moral education is a sheer absurdity, unless there is a moral nature or conscience that postulates moral law and obligation as necessary and universal truths; and that, too, antecedent to all possible teaching as to what is and is not morally right or wrong in the life.

The ideas of conscience, then, are by no means prejudices of education; it is impossible that they should be. They are irresistible intuitions of our very nature, and lie developed in the moral reason or conscience as laws and principles, in the light of which education on moral subjects, as touching the activities of life, is possible.

But how, then, are the ideas of conscience developed? Instrumentally, no doubt, they are developed by some experience. We experience pleasure or pain. This experience of pleasure or pain is the condition of developing in the reason that which is valuable to being for its own sake, and the evil, or that which is naturally evil on its own account to a moral being. Happiness is affirmed to be intrinsically valuable, or a good; misery as intrinsically an evil. The ideas of natural good and evil develop in the conscience the affirmation that the good ought to be chosen for its own sake, and that the evil ought never to be chosen for its own sake, and only as a condition of good; and these affirmations are developed in the universal form as necessary and universal truths, or in the form of moral law—that the good of universal being ought to be chosen by moral agents for its own sake, and that misery ought to be universally avoided, except as a condition of good. The law is also extended naturally to the lives of all moral agents; and the conscience postulates irresistibly that all moral agents ought to devote themselves to the promotion of the highest good of universal being, and consequently to avoid as far as possible the introduction of misery. This affirmation of conscience is made upon condition of the intuitive perception of a moral relation existing between the choice and the good of being—that such is the nature of good and such the nature of choice, that it is morally fit that the good should be chosen for its own sake. Upon the perception by the conscience of this moral relation between choice and its object, the affirmation is developed that it is right to choose, or in other words, that choice ought to terminate on the good, and that we and all moral agents ought to choose the good and therein refuse the evil.

The perception, then, of that which is naturally good, to wit, the blessedness or happiness of being, develops in the conscience the conception of the morally good, or of virtue. Natural good being perceived by the natural reason or happiness being affirmed by the natural reason to be a good in itself, conscience thereupon affirms that moral good or virtue consists in the disinterested choice of natural good or happiness. Thus the idea of moral good is developed in the conscience by the intuition of natural good in the intrinsically valuable to being by natural reason.

The condition, then, of the development of the ideas of conscience, is the experience of pleasure or happiness. In an animal, this experience does not suggest the idea of the intrinsically valuable, and consequently of moral law and obligation to choose it; but in rational beings, the experience of happiness and its opposite at a very early age develops the idea of the good or valuable whereupon the moral nature simultaneously affirms moral law, moral obligation, right, wrong, virtue, vice, good and ill desert. It is not so much my object in this place to state the exact order in which these truths are developed in the conscience, as the condition of their development. It will be observed that in the development of these ideas of conscience we assume necessarily and irresistibly our moral agency, the freedom of our will, the existence and rightful authority of God, his moral perfections, and that he requires of us conformity to this law which conscience imposes on us in his name.

So it should be remembered that obligation is always invoked in the name of God; and we cannot resist the conviction that he requires of us that which our conscience affirms that we ought to do. If we consider the matter as revealed in consciousness, we shall perceive that obligation in us implies two parties, one under obligation and one to whom obligation is due; that we do not affirm moral obligation to ourselves nor to society, but to God as our rightful lawgiver. Hence the Psalmist affirms that he had sinned against God only. We cannot possibly regard this obligation as imposed by society, or by any other being than God. The will of no being but God can be moral law. We cannot conceive of moral obligation, then, in any other light than as an obligation to God; and in affirming this obligation we necessarily assume his existence, his moral attributes, relations, and his moral perfections, as conditions of our obligation to obey him.

LECTURE V.

INTRODUCTORY.
THE UNDERSTANDING, JUDGMENT, AND FREEDOM OF THE WILL.

I. THE UNDERSTANDING.

In further remarking upon the revelations given in consciousness, I call attention again to THE UNDERSTANDING as a function of the intellect. This faculty is concerned with the physical as distinct from the metaphysical, or with things in distinction from ideas. It combines, as has been before said, the intuitions of sense and of the other intellectual functions, and forms notions of things. It is concerned with the concrete and contingent, the finite, facts, and events. I have observed that much confusion arises from confounding the intuitions of reason with understanding conceptions. For example, in the understanding conception of God, the attributes of infinity and perfection are dropped; of God as the absolute or unconditioned, the infinite and perfect, the understanding has no conception, these being attributes incognizable by this faculty. It can have a conception of God as a concrete existence, indefinitely great, and of all his attributes as realities, but of no one of them can it conceive the attribute of infinity, except in the Lockean sense of finding no limit. But this is only the indefinite. In understanding conceptions, therefore, of God, I plainly perceive in consciousness that I refer to God my understanding conception of myself, only I conceive of him as being indefinitely greater than myself. I find that with my understanding I cannot but conceive of God as being an agent, and a moral agent like myself. I conceive of him as a personality, as having will, intellect, and sensibility. I conceive of him with my understanding as an affectionate Father, as a lawgiver, judge—in short, with my understanding I conceive of God in a manner that brings him into relation to me that is approachable and endearing. But if with my understanding I attempt to conceive of God's eternity or infinity, I find a seeming contradiction between my understanding and my rational conception. So of everything that is infinite.

My understanding conception of time is that of constant flux or succession of moments; my rational conception is that of an infinite unit, or duration as a unit. This is real time. It is absolute duration. Now my understanding conception of God is a very different one from my rational one in regard to his eternity. With my understanding I cannot conceive of an existence above the conditions of time and space. Everything given by the understanding is necessarily given under these conditions. Consequently my understanding conception of him is not as the self-existent and eternal Being, but simply as an agent living on through time as we do, of whom may be predicated, here and there, time, past, present, and future. From the very nature of the understanding it can conceive of God only under these limitations. But my rational conception of God is that, in some respects, he differs infinitely from this my understanding notion or conception of him. Then, the reason supplies what is inadequate in the understanding conception.

The rational conception is, of God the unconditioned, and of course as above conditions of time and space. The rational conception gives him as the infinite Being; consequently, that in respect to him there can be no here or there. With respect to all other beings there can be, and must be, place; but to the infinite Being, so far as his own existence is concerned, there can be no place in the sense of here or there; for here implies there, and the term here has no meaning unless there is a there, and there unless there is a here. These are terms of distinction that cannot belong to God. Of all other beings he can say here and there; but of himself there is neither here nor there, for this would contradict his infinity or omnipresence.

Now I find in my consciousness that in this respect my understanding and my reason differ entirely in their conceptions of God. The same is true of time as it respects God. Being absolute, or above the condition of time, or which is the same thing, being self-existent, he can sustain no such relations to time as finite beings must. So far as his infinite being is concerned, there can be neither past, present, nor future; for present as distinguished from past or future implies the past and the future. But my rational conception of God is that he is above conditions of time. Indeed, to call this in question is deny that he is self-existent, and to say that he never can exist. But this entirely baffles my understanding conception of him. My understanding cannot possibly conceive of him as being in such a sense above the conditions of time and place that it is not strictly proper to predicate of him both time and place. Hence we speak of him as everywhere, as here and there. This is common language both in the Bible and in all that we say of him. We also speak of him as sustaining relations to time such as we sustain. Especially in this—we speak of all time as being present to him.

Such language is inevitable as expressing our understanding conceptions of God, and these conceptions are not deletions in an injurious sense. And yet they fall infinitely short of expressing the rational conception that we have of God. Our understanding conception of God is that he fills all things; and the understanding is even overwhelmed by the magnitude of the universe, and get its most exalted conception of his greatness by conceiving of him as being everywhere and as pervading the whole universe. But the rational conception of God is that he is infinitely above all ages, time, cycles, and our understanding conceptions of time. Care should therefore always be taken to discriminate between the rational conceptions of God and the understanding conceptions of him. The rational conception gives the idea of his being a substance possessing certain attributes; and that of infinity and perfection, absoluteness and incomprehensibility are attributes of his. The reason must necessarily conceive of him as a unity; the understanding may conceive of him as a three-fold personality.

II. THE JUDGMENT.

Again, I must add a few remarks concerning the judgment as a function of the intellect. This faculty is concerned with evidence and proof. It is the faculty largely concerned in logical processes of thought. In consciousness I find that it is a passive function of the intellect, in the sense that when certain conditions are fulfilled, its decisions are inevitable. And yet, in regard to these conditions, I find in consciousness that by willing I direct attention either to or away from the proper sources of evidence in any case to be decided; and the bias of my will I find has often a decided influence in the view taken by the judgment of what is or is not true. By consciousness I find that I often prejudge a case in consequence of the unfair attitude of my will—that often I am unwilling to be convinced of certain truths or facts; or on the other had am very desirous of being convinced that certain things are true. In this case I perceive in consciousness that I cannot trust my opinions or the decisions of my judgment where my will is in a committed attitude; and I often discover that I have been deceived by the committed and uncandid position of my will. I find also in my consciousness that my conscience holds me responsible in many cases for the decisions of my judgment as well as for the actions of my life. It forbids me to judge censoriously or unfairly of my neighbor. It condemns me for prejudice universally; and conscience I perceive will hold me responsible, not only for the decisions of my judgment in all cases of doubt, but for my acts, whether in accordance with my judgment or not.

Conscience, I perceive, will not allow me to deceive myself in the decisions of my judgment, and then take refuge under these delusions to justify myself. In consciousness I perceive that conscience will justify my conduct only as I am conscious of judging and action in a perfectly benevolent state of mind. In consciousness I find that I am as severely censured by conscience for prejudice against my neighbor as I am for any injury that I might outwardly inflict upon him. Nay, so far as my own conscience is concerned, I perceive that to think ill of my neighbor is often to do him the greatest injury of which I am capable. His character is dear to himself and to God. Nothing in the outward life can be so valuable, and no injustice to him can be so great as in my judgment unreasonably to rob him of his character. Christ in his teaching strongly reprobates prejudice, and insists that all our judgments shall be formed in strictest charity. In the looseness of men's thoughts it often appears as if their ideas of morality were confined very much to their outward actions and relations, and as if they deemed it a greater crime to defraud a man in a business transaction than to judge his character uncharitably. But by attending to the voice of conscience as revealed in consciousness, we shall see that prejudice against a man, that allowing ourselves to form censorious judgments, is a far greater injustice to him than the mere defrauding him of money; and that publishing a censorious judgment and uttering a slander of a neighbor is one of the greatest of earthly crimes against him. Indeed, there is almost nothing in which we more frequently sin than in the use of this intellectual function, the judgment; and it is amazing to see to what extent sins of this character, though of the deepest dye, are overlooked in our estimate of our moral condition.

III. THE WILL.

But I must pass in the next place to some additional remarks upon the will, as this faculty and its activities are revealed in consciousness. By the will is intended that power or faculty of the mind by which I act. And here it is requisite to say, that by power or faculty is not intended a member, as we speak of the body as divided into parts and member; but by faculty is intended a property of the mind, a capacity, or that of which the mind is capable or susceptible. It has been said that the mind is to be regarded as a unit possessing a variety of capacities and susceptibilities. By the will is intended the mind's innate power of choice. It is the will in which particularly personality resides. By this power we are made agents, that is, self-active beings. By this power, in connection with the intellect and sensibility, we are made moral agents, or morally responsible actors. By this power we are self-determining in regard to our own activity, and sovereigns of our own actions. We mean by the freedom of the will precisely this: That we direct and decide our own choices entirely above and beyond the law of necessity. When I choose I find that I am universally conscious that I elect, prefer one course to the other, or one object to the other; and that in the identical circumstances in which I choose I am able in every instance to choose the opposite of what in fact I do choose. Herein, and nowhere else, I perceive the liberty of my will to reside.

Some have defined the freedom of the will to consist in our ability to execute our volitions, or to do as we will. But herein is no liberty. I am conscious that it is the law of necessity by which the actions of my will and the actions of my muscles are connected. My muscles cannot neglect or refuse to move under the decisions of my will. If in any case they do not obey my will, it is because this law of connection is for the time suspended. But it is absurd to define human liberty as consisting in the ability, power, or opportunity to execute my choices, or to do in conformity with my willing. I cannot but execute my volitions unless some obstacle is opposed to their execution that overcomes the power of my will. The willing is the doing inwardly; and this inward doing must express itself in outward doing by a necessary law. I cannot act otherwise than as I will. Of all this I am conscious.

I know, then, by certain knowledge that I am an agent, a free, self-active being; and I know this with a certainty that cannot be shaken by logic or sophistry. I find that I cannot but assume my own liberty of will in every instance of affirmed obligation. Indeed, I find it impossible to conceive of an obligation to act, only as I have power thus to will and choose to act. And I find that I cannot conceive of obligation, of praise or blame, where but one kind of action is possible. If there is no other way, but so or so I must act, and it is impossible for me to act in any other direction or way, I cannot conceive myself as morally responsible in such a case.

In considering the question I perceive that my reason affirms that this liberty of will is essential to moral agency; that forced action is not responsible action; and that any action of will determined by a law of necessity cannot be moral action. I am conscious of affirming that where liberty of will ends and necessity begins, there moral agency ends; and that moral agency implies the power to resist any degree of motive presented as an inducement to act. If at any point the considerations presented could force the will, that forced act is not the act of a moral agent. Moral agency ceased where force commenced.

In consciousness I also perceive that as a moral agent my liberty is regarded even by God as sacred; he does not, and will not invade it. He knocks at the door of my heart; but he does not break in. He pleads, commands, and reasons; but he does not force. He will not invade the sanctuary of my liberty, nor allow it to be done by any creature in the universe. In this respect I conceive myself as bearing his image. I cannot but so regard myself. I am a free moral agent as he is; and this image in me he respects as his own image. This image with him is sacred; he will never invade the sanctuary which he himself has created, of my own personal liberty. He will present considerations to induce me to imitate him in action; but to force me to act like himself is naturally impossible and involves a contradiction; for forced action would not be like his action, his action being always free.

I find myself, therefore, necessarily conceiving of him as holding me responsible for the actions of my will; but never controlling these actions by any law of necessity or force. By consciousness I find that I affirm that this must be true of all moral agents, and that this liberty of will is necessarily implied in the very conception of a moral agent. Thus I know myself; and this knowledge is so intuitive and irresistible that I can no more doubt my moral agency and moral responsibility in respect to the actions of my will than I can doubt my own existence.

Again, by the use of the faculty of will I am conscious of being a cause, of causing the acts of will directly, and then indirectly actions of my body; and through the body of causing changes in the material universe around me. By the actions of my will I am also conscious of exhibiting my ideas to others, and of being instrumental in influencing the minds around me; and by influencing their minds I influence their bodies; and by influencing their bodies I produce many changes in the material universe with which I and they stand connected. I am conscious in willing, of being a proper cause. I say, in willing I cause my acts of will directly, and whatever else I cause, I cause by an act of my will. In willing, I act. I cause these actions of will, and am myself a proper cause. Proper cause must be me. Acts of will are not properly cause, for they are caused by the responsible agent. They are only instrumental causes, as are the hands or other faculties of body or mind. I act; in acting I am a cause, that is, my acts are effects. In consciousness I perceive that I am a cause, and I also perceive that reason affirms God to be a cause, and to be a first cause, and that in the most strict and proper sense a cause.

In consciousness I learn that the freedom of the will does not imply power to abstain from all action or choice in the presence of objects of choice; but in the power of preference, choosing the one or the other in a sovereign manner. I further learn in consciousness that I cannot choose without an object of choice; and that objects of choice are merely conditions upon which it is possible to choose. But that objects of choice do not necessitate or compel choice in the direction of the object. Without some object I cannot choose at all. But in the presence of any object I can choose one way or the other; I can prefer the existence or non-existence of the object in a sovereign manner.

I perceive, then, in consciousness, that what are generally termed motives are the conditions of action, but never the causes of action. The object is that without which I cannot choose at all; but in the presence of the object I may choose it or refuse it. Again, I learn in consciousness that the object of choice is something in which I can conceive there is some intrinsic or relative value. I perceive that it is contrary to my nature, for example, to choose evil either moral or natural, that is, sin or misery for its own sake. To choose anything for its own sake is to choose it for that which is intrinsic, and on its own account. But I can see nothing in sin, nothing in misery that is not intrinsically abhorrent to my own being; therefore I find that it is not to me an object of ultimate choice—I cannot choose it for its own sake. By consciousness I find that I remain indifferent to any object present to my mind in which I perceive nothing valuable or injurious, intrinsically or relatively, to any being in the universe. In such a case no matter what the object might be, I am necessarily as indifferent, so far as choice is concerned, as to a mathematical point. It is to me, and can be to me, no object demanding or even admitting of choice. I cannot prefer its existence or its non-existence, for I can conceive no possible reason for this preference. The preference in such a case would be an act of the will without an object, which is a natural impossibility.

The freedom of the will, then, does not imply the power to abstain from all choice in the presence of a real object of choice; nor does it consist in the power to choose without an object of choice; nor in the power to discriminate between the objects of choice where the mind can perceive no reason for discrimination. If the mind can perceive no difference in any respect between one object and another, neither in respect to what is intrinsic or relative in the object, the will cannot prefer the one to the other; for this is a contradiction, it would be a choice having no object. If two objects be presented to the mind, one of which I am to choose, if these objects are in all respects precisely similar in my estimation, I can choose the one and be indifferent to the other, but I cannot prefer the one to the other; for this again would imply a preference without an object, or any conceivable reason for the preference.

Again, in consciousness I learn that certain things are abhorrent to my whole nature, so far as their intrinsic nature and character are concerned; and as such they are not objects of choice. I can refuse them, but choose them for their own sake I cannot. And again, I perceive that other things commend themselves to my nature in the sense of being objects of desire. I can desire them on their own account, that is, for what they are in themselves; or, I can desire them on account of their relations to other desirable things. And I perceive, that to be an object of choice, a thing, as I have already said, must appear to me to be of some relative, or of some intrinsic value. If it be an object either intrinsically or relatively valuable, or the opposite, either intrinsically or relatively evil, the will can act, and must act, in the presence of it. If it be regarded as intrinsically evil, the will cannot choose it for its own sake, but necessarily rejects it. And where there is such a necessary rejection, this rejection is not a moral act. I learn by circumstances that what I regard as intrinsically evil, such as sin or misery, can only be chooses as relatively an object of desire. I can desire the infliction of pain upon another either in accordance with my ideas of justice, or to gratify a feeling of resentment. But the thing that I wish here particularly to insist upon is, that the freedom of the will does not imply the ability to choose things that are to us no objects of choice, in the sense that they in any respect commend themselves either to the intellect or to the sensibility; that no state of the sensibility can desire, and no function of the intellect can affirm, that in any respect they are a good. In consciousness I learn that my will sustains such a relation to my intellect on the one hand, and to my sensibility on the other, that from each of these departments of my mind I receive the motives that are conditions of my will's actions.

It appears to me that philosophers have greatly erred in maintaining that the will never acts except in obedience to desire. I am conscious that this is not true; and that I often act in opposition to all conscious desire. It has been common for philosophers to maintain that no presentations merely through the intellect excite the will's activity, or supply the conditions of its action; but that the will universally is dependent upon the excitement in the sensibility of some appetite, feeling or desire; and that whenever it acts it always obeys some desire. Now to this I object, first, that in my own case I am conscious that it is not true; that the moral law as given by my conscience is to me a rule of action; that it supplies the condition of the will's activity that I cannot but act in its presence whether there is desire or no desire, or whatever the desire may be. The law itself as subjectively revealed in my intellect actually necessitates action one way or the other, and my liberty consists in acting in accordance with or in opposition to this affirmed subjective law. This I as really know as I know my own existence. But secondly, I object to the doctrine in question, that if the will acts in obedience to desire, its actions are either sinful, or they have no moral character at all. Universally, feeling, desire, emotion, and all the states of the sensibility are blind. They are never the law or rule of action. The will ought never to act in conformity with them except as the law of the intelligence dictates that course of action; and in that case the virtue consists in its obeying the dictates of the intelligence, or the law, and not in its obeying the blind desire, which is never law. Indeed, herein is the distinction between saints and sinners; sinners obey their desires and saints their convictions. In other words, sinners follow the impulses of their sensibility, and to gratify them is their adopted law; but saints obey conscience, or the law of God as postulated by the conscience. I am conscious of this in my own case; and that when I act in accordance with the convictions of my conscience, I often at the same time act in opposition to the feelings of my sensibility. Indeed, in precisely this consists the Christian warfare —in resisting the emotional and sensitive parts of our nature and not indulging the desires, appetites, and propensities, but in obeying the law of God as postulated and given in the conscience.

I regard the theory that the will never acts except in obedience to desire as eminently false and dangerous, contrary to consciousness, and contrary to any sound view of moral obligation or moral action. In consciousness I find the distinction plainly marked that my conscience or reason is the law-giving faculty, the decisions of which I am bound to obey, consulting the desires of the sensibility no farther than this consulting and gratifying of the sensibility is dictated and required by the conscience.

I perceive that Bishop Butler in his sermons affirms that virtue consists in obeying certain desires. He says that we have constitutionally the desire of our own good and happiness and the desire for the happiness of others. We have private desires and public desires; that is, desires for private good and desires for public good; that virtue consists in the gratification of these public desires; and he regards it virtuous thus to choose because the desire itself is virtuous. He thinks that the nature of the desire gives character to the choice to gratify it, or makes it virtuous to act in conformity with it. But I do not so read the convictions of my own mind. Constitutional desire is never virtuous or vicious. Desire as distinct from willing, or choice, or volition, has, and can have, no moral character. The desires for the public good are passive; and this Bishop Butler holds, if I understand him. They can therefore in no proper sense be virtuous or vicious desires; and to obey them is not virtue, or to disobey them is not vice. To choose the public good for its intrinsic value is virtue; but to choose it for its intrinsic value as affirmed by the reason is not to choose it because it is desired. To refuse the public good is sin, because we intuitively affirm that it ought to be chosen for its own sake and not to be refused. But the sin does not lie in denying the desire, but in refusing to obey the law of God as postulated in the conscience. It is true that the conscience could not affirm obligation to choose the public good except upon the condition that it is regarded as a good, and that experience of pleasure or pain in the sensibility is the chronological antecedent and the condition of our having the idea of the good or the valuable.

Our desire, therefore, may be the condition of our affirming moral obligation in the sense that they are the condition of developing the idea of the valuable, and therefore the idea of the obligation to choose the valuable for its own sake. But in reading my own consciousness I cannot perceive that the conditions of my will's actions are the excitement of desire, and that virtue or vice consists in acting either in conformity with or against desire apart from the law of my intelligence or conscience. I suppose that animals act purely under the influence of the sensibility. They have no other rule of action. We are under moral law, moral law as given by conscience; and whatever the states of the sensibility are, we affirm ourselves bound to obey the rule of life revealed in the conscience.

In my own case I am sure that conscience requires me to act simply in view of the motive as presented in the law; that in the presence of that motive, whether I have desires or not, I am bound to act, and must act, and I do act one way or the other, and am held responsible accordingly. I am conscious that it often happens that desire and feeling are in accordance with the rule of duty. In such cases it is a comfort and a pleasure to decide and act in accordance with the rule of duty as given in conscience, and the performance of duty becomes a pleasure; but it is neither the pleasure nor the pain that results from obeying God or the law of my conscience. It is neither the gratification nor the denial of my desires that is the rule of my duty. This rule I receive from my intellect. My sensibility is to be consulted in my moral activity only as its emotions, desires and states are in accordance with the dictates of my conscience; or in other words, only as my conscience commands me to deny or refuse their indulgence.

A recent writer professes to believe in the freedom of the will; and yet his definition of what constitutes freedom of the will is so equivocal that I cannot understand why he should regard himself as believing in the freedom of the will in any proper sense.[5] His

---

[5] Mental Philosophy: Including the Intellect, Sensibilities, and Will, by Joseph Haven, D.D., Prof. of Systematic Theology in the Theological Seminary,

definition of freedom of the will is in substance, the power to will as we please. But it may be asked, what does this mean? What does this writer mean by "please?" Does he mean to use the word "please" or "pleasure" here in the sense of a voluntary state of mind? Is it willing or choice? If so, then the power to will as we please is simply the power to will as we will. But have we power to will as we do not will? To say that we have power to will as we really do will is nothing to the purpose. Or, does he mean in this case that we have power to will otherwise than we do will? Does he mean to say that we will as we do will by our own power; or that our pleasure, or some state of mind which he calls pleasure, necessitates the act of willing or choice? If by his definition he means simply that we have power to will as we in fact do will, this is nothing to the purpose, unless he also adds and holds that in the very identical case and under the identical circumstances we have power to will the opposite of what we do really will.

Secondly, Or, by "please" does he mean that we have power to will as we desire? If this is what he means, I ask, Have we power to will against desire? and against the strongest desire? If we have not power to will any otherwise than as we desire, and in accordance with the strongest desire, then is not our will free. But does he mean that any degree of desire is sufficient as a condition of our having power to will? That we have power to will against the strongest desire and in accordance with the weakest desire? But that desire is really an essential condition of our power to will? If this is his meaning, I would inquire whether the known command of God can impose obligation to will unless it creates desire in the sensibility in accordance with it? If desire is an essential condition of the power to will, it must be an essential condition of obligation to will; and in no case can we be under obligation until a desire is created in the sensibility in the direction of the thing required. But would this writer maintain that a plain command of God could impose no obligation unless it created a corresponding desire in the sensibility? Would this writer maintain that the direct affirmation of conscience imposes no obligation until it creates desire in the

Chicago, Ill., and Late Prof. of Intellectual and Moral Philosophy in Amherst College; page 515; first edition, 1857.

sensibility? Now if this doctrine be true, that desire is an indispensable condition of obligation, conscience cannot affirm obligation until after the desire really exists. If there is in fact no ability to will till desire in the sensibility is awakened by a necessary law—for desire we certainly know to be passive and not free—it then follows that the will is not free to act except in obedience to desires that are created by a law of necessity. When desire is awakened by necessity, I would ask this writer, does he mean to say that in every instance the will can act not only as we please or desire, but contrary to our desire or our pleasure? For this is the real question.

To be free, the will must have power in every case of moral obligation to act one way or the other in a sovereign manner. It must have power to act either in the presence of conviction or the perception of obligation, whatever the desire may be, or whether there be any desire or not; or it must be unable so to choose. If it is unable so to choose, it is not free. But if able so to choose simply under the perception of obligation, and without reference to desire or against desire, then it is free, otherwise it is not.

But again, ability to choose in a required direction must be a condition of obligation to choose in that direction. If the will has not power, then, to choose against desire, however strong that desire may be, there can be no obligation to choose against that desire; and obligation must invariably be as the desire is. If we are unable to will against the strongest desire, we can be under no obligation to will against that desire.

Again, if we always of necessity act in accordance with the strongest desire, then it follows either that there is no obligation, because the will is not free; or that we always do our duty, for obligation and ability must always be coincident. But again, does this writer mean by the word "please" that which we affirm to be right or useful? Does he mean to say that we have power to choose as we see or as we feel that we ought to choose? If this is what he means, then I would ask, if we have power at the same time and under the identical circumstances to choose as we see and feel that we ought not to choose? If not, the will is not free.

Again, does this writer mean that we have power to will according to the sense of what is upon the whole most agreeable?

This is Edwards' view. He maintained that we have power to will according to the sense of the most agreeable; or more strictly, that we cannot help so willing. And strictly, he maintained that this sense of the most agreeable and the choice or willing are identical. With Edwards, this sense of the most agreeable, which is identical with the choice itself, is necessitated by the presence of certain motives. Now is this what this writer means? Is he Edwardean? This he does not profess. But is not his definition, after all, identical in its real meaning with that of Edwards?

But if this writer means by please or pleasure that we have power to choose that which is most pleasing to us, what does he mean by its being most pleasing? Does he or does he not mean, that which upon the whole seems most agreeable to us? If this is so, does he mean that we have power to choose the opposite of that which seems most agreeable to us? Do we by necessity choose that which is most agreeable? If so, this is not freedom of the will.

But again, I wish to ask, Is this pleasing or pleasure, according to which he says we have power to will, a state of the sensibility, and therefore passive? Or is it a voluntary state, and therefore an act of the will? If it is a voluntary state, it is identical with choice, and comes to this—that we have power to choose as we do choose. But if this is all, this is not freedom of will. But if this being pleased or pleasure is a state of the sensibility, then the question returns, Have we power to will in opposition to it? Again, if we have power to will only as we please, and by please is intended a state of the sensibility, and this state of the sensibility being passive is produced by a law of necessity, how is the will free? It is not. Indeed, if I understand this writer, his view of the freedom of the will amounts to nothing. He has by no means discussed the real question of freedom of the will. He has by no means stated it, nor does he by any means hold it.

Edwards professed to hold the freedom of the will, but gave such a definition of what constitutes freedom of the will as not at all to discuss the real question. His idea of freedom of will is power or ability to do as we please; or in other words, to execute our pleasure, or to act in accordance with our sense of the most agreeable, which sense of the most agreeable is identical with willing or volition. Now with him pure opportunity or ability to do as we will is liberty of will. But this is no liberty of will, for we cannot do otherwise than as we will. Edwards denied that we could originate in a sovereign manner our own volitions or actions of will. With him, this sense of the most agreeable, which is identical with volition, is necessitated by the objective motive. With him we are only free to do, but not free to will. That is, we are free to do, with him, when we are able to execute our volitions; but our volitions themselves are necessitated. But this is only freedom in the outward act, and not in the act of the will at all. But it was the freedom of the will that he professed to discuss, when in fact by his definition he evaded the whole inquiry. According to him there is no real freedom in any case, even in the outward act; for he did not pretend that our outward acts were not necessitated by the actions of our will. It is therefore absurd to maintain that freedom can belong to the mere acts of the body, which acts, as plainly revealed to us in consciousness, are necessitated by the will. With Edwards, then, man is not an agent in any proper sense of the term. An agent must be a self-determiner; otherwise he is a mere instrument or machine, determined not by a power within himself but by something presented to him as a motive of action. He denied and even ridiculed the idea of self-determination in man or in any other being, even in God himself. I say ridiculed, because by his mode of reasoning he represented the idea of self-determination as really ridiculous, and yet maintained the freedom of the will. This is absurd and preposterous.

Now what does this recent writer, Professor Haven, mean by asserting that we have power to will as we please? Perhaps I do not understand him. But if I do understand him, his definition of freedom of the will is radically defective, and he does not maintain the freedom of the will.

But the freedom of the will is a necessary knowledge, assumed by us as the radical condition of affirming our obligation. In every instance of affirming obligation the condition of this affirmation is the assumption or knowledge, or if you please, the consciousness, that we have power to will or choose as we affirm the obligation to choose. First, I appeal to consciousness—that we are directly conscious of assuming in every case of affirmed obligation that we can will in accordance with the obligation or in opposition to it in the identical circumstances in which we affirm the obligation. Secondly, in every instance of affirmed obligation we are conscious that this knowledge of our ability to will in accordance with obligation is a condition of our affirming the obligation; and that for the assumption of our ability we could not conceive it possible that we should be under any such obligation. This is certainly an ultimate fact in consciousness, and not to be set aside by logic. No truth of consciousness, no affirmation of the pure reason or intuition of any intuitive faculty is ever to be invalidated by any logical process. Intuitive knowledge is the most certain of all knowledge, and lies at the foundation of all knowledge. Our reasonings are often fallacious because of the errors to which the judgment is liable; our intuitions cannot deceive us. Therefore, the freedom of the will rests upon the same basis with the knowledge of our existence. We are just as certain that we are under moral obligation as we are that we exist. We are as certain that moral obligation respects acts of will as that we exist. We are as certain that the will is free, or that we have power to will in accordance with obligation or in opposition to it, as we are that we are under obligation, or that we exist at all.

But why blink, or why evade the real question of the freedom of the will? Why call the will free, to conceive the possibility of obligation, and yet so to define the freedom as to leave the question a mere mockery to a moral agent. It is undeniable that moral obligation is obligation to choose the highest good of universal being as an end, and to put forth those volitions that are possible to us and in our estimation useful to secure that end. Now this obligation implies the power to put forth these acts of will. Why then not march up at once to the definition of freedom of will—that it consists in the power to choose or refuse in every case of moral obligation?

But again, what is essential to obligation? Is obligation created by the perception of that object which we affirm we ought to choose? For example, is obligation to benevolence affirmed simply in view of the intrinsic value of the good of universal being? Or must there be a desire existing for this good as the condition of the obligation? Must both the perception of the intrinsic value of the good exist, and also desire in the sensibility in the same direction, as conditions of moral obligation? If both the perception and the desire must exist as the conditions of our power to choose the good of being, then the obligation cannot exist simply in view of the intrinsic and infinite value of the good. But desire must exist; and if desire fails to exist, however clear the perception of the intrinsic value of the good, obligation is not affirmed. Obligation does not exist because power does not exist to will in that direction. In this case the conscience must wait when the good is discovered, however clearly it is perceived, until desire awakes in the sensibility, before it can affirm the obligation to choose.

But will anyone seriously pretend that either God or conscience must wait before affirming obligation till desire for the object which we ought to choose is awakened? Who does not know the contrary? How long shall philosophers hold that ability to choose is conditioned upon awakened desire; and yet maintain, or seem to maintain, that obligation exists even in opposition to desire, or whether desire exists or not?

LECTURE VI.

INTRODUCTORY
IMMORTALITY OF THE SOUL.

I. ARGUMENT FROM CONSCIOUSNESS.

1. WE have seen that in consciousness man knows his own existence. He knows himself as a spiritual being inhabiting a material body; that is, he is aware of possessing and exercising the attributes or powers of a spirit as distinct from the attributes or qualities of a material body. Consciousness directly gives his spirituality, and sense gives to consciousness the intuitive knowledge of our bodies. I think, I feel, I will; these are not acts or qualities of matter. Matter has extension, form, solidity, impenetrability, inertia; but these are not properties or qualities of mind. Spirit has not extension, solidity, inertia. Spirit is not a space-filling substance. This we know to be true, for God is a Spirit and is omnipresent; and if spirit were a space-filling substance, the existence of God would be incompatible with the existence of anything else.

I am conscious as a spirit of using my body as its instrument, but I am conscious that my body is not myself, my thinking, willing substance. I am sure by sense that I have a body, and by consciousness I am sure that I have a mind.

2. In consciousness I am aware that I am an agent, and not a mere instrument. I act from myself, that is, my mind is self-active; and my body has no power of action only as I move the self-activity of my mind. In consciousness I know that as a mind I am a cause; not merely in the sense of a secondary cause, or in the sense of transmitting by a law of necessity an impulse which I receive by the same law. I know that as mind I am sovereign in my activity, and that I do not belong to the chain of material causes and effects that comprise the material universe around me. As a mind I am conscious of being apart from this chain of material cause and effect, above it, and that I have power in a great many

ways to act upon it and modify the order in which these causes and effects would otherwise flow.

3. In consciousness I know myself as a free agent. I not only have the power of self-activity, that is, do not merely act from myself and of myself; but I act in one direction or another at my sovereign discretion—the manner in which I shall act being determined by myself, and by no agency in the universe but my own.

4. In consciousness I know myself to be an intelligent agent. That is, I reason, judge, and act in view of all considerations which are present to my mind. In other words, I am aware in consciousness that I assign to myself reasons for my actions, and act upon the condition of their presence to my intellect.

5. In consciousness I know myself as a moral agent. I have a conscience; I am under moral government and moral law, perform moral actions and have a moral character. All this I know by direct consciousness. My existence, then, as such a being, is a fact of consciousness. The question at present is not how I came to exist; the fact that I do exist is the question immediately before us. We have seen it to be a first truth of reason that every event must have a cause, that is, of a cause, an adequate cause. Now it follows that whatever exists will continue to exist forever, unless by some adequate cause it is annihilated. All existences are therefore naturally immortal in the sense that when existence is once given, they will continue to exist forever unless they are annihilated.

Some have maintained that nothing exists in such a sense that it would continue to exist for a moment if not continued in existence by a divine upholding. But pray what can be intended by this? Suppose the divine upholding to be withdrawn—is it intended that all existences except God have in themselves the law of self-annihilation? That were God to withdraw his support they would by a law of their own nature annihilate themselves? Surely this is gratuitous, and even absurd. To say that anything can annihilate itself is certainly a contradiction. What then does the assertion mean, that nothing save God continues to exist except by a divine upholding? Is it intended that if God withdraws himself from the existences that make up the universe, they will sink into annihilation of themselves? But how can this be? If there are real existences in the universe that are not God, if they are ever annihilated, it must be by some positive influence adequate to such a result.

I do not see why the philosophy that everything exists only as it is divinely held up into existence does not amount to pantheism. It seems to me equivalent to maintaining that all existences are only forms and modes of divine existence; and that if you abstract that which is divine from all existences there is nothing left. To claim, then, for the soul of man immortality in the sense of endless existence, is to claim for it no more than justly be claimed for all real existences, unless they are by divine power annihilated.

6. If anyone affirms that the soul of man is not immortal, the burden of proof is upon him. Certainly it is immortal in its nature, that is, it has a real existence and cannot pass out of existence without being annihilated by some power out of and above itself; and so far as we can see, by some power equivalent to that which gave it being. If then it be contended that the soul of man is mortal, it must be proven that an adequate power will be exerted to annihilate it. The burden of proof upon the question of the soul's immortality does not belong to Christians but to those who deny its immortality. It does exist; it must continue to exist unless annihilated.

It will not be contended that any being but God can annihilate it—will God annihilate it? Is there any proof that he ever does annihilate a soul? Of course, in this part of our inquiry we are not consulting the Scriptures, for the question of their divine authority has not yet been mooted by us in this course of study. We inquire, therefore, on principles of science and in the light of natural reason. What reason is there for supposing that the soul of man will ever be annihilated? Certainly the dissolution of the body affords no reason to believe that the soul is annihilated. The body is not annihilated, but only changes its form. Indeed we know not that anything that has had an existence ever has been or ever will be annihilated. Material bodies we know to be perpetually changing their form, because they are perpetually changing the particles of which they are composed. Personal identity cannot strictly, we know, be affirmed of our bodies for any two moments of our lives. All the particles of organized being are in a state of perpetual flux. This is a fact of science. But this is not true of our spiritual nature. Our spiritual nature is not an organized substance. It is spirit, not composed of particles, not a space-filling substance; and the changes in the body we know do not interfere with the personal identity of the soul.

7. The mortality of the body is admitted, and adequate causes to change its form are known to exist. But this is by no means true of the mind. I know it has been affirmed that the mind is after all material, and that thought, volition, and feeling, are only results of refined cerebral organization. But has this ever been proved? It is mere assertion. And do those who make such assertions expect them to be received? The soul as known to us possesses none of the qualities of matter; it is therefore gratuitous and even absurd to affirm its materiality. To say that when the body is dissolved, the mind disappears, is only to prove that the body is the organ of the mind's manifestation in this state of existence; and of this we are conscious. Of course, when the material body decays, the mind has lost the medium by which it communicated with other minds inhabiting material bodies; and this is all that is implied in the fact that the mind ceases to manifest itself when the body is decayed. It is by means of our bodies that we reveal ourselves to those that inhabit bodies like ourselves. When our bodies are dissolved, the medium of this revelation has ceased to exist, and consequently the mind inhabiting the body has no longer power to manifest itself to those that are in bodies. We know of no such medium.

II. MORAL ARGUMENT.

1. We have just said that we are conscious of a moral nature, or conscience; that we posses the attributes of moral agents and are subjects of moral government; that moral law is revealed in our own consciousness, affirmed by our own conscience as an authoritative rule of action; and that moral obligation is imposed on us in the name of God. The first truth, accountability, implies this—that conscience legislates for God.

2. We also know in consciousness that we irresistibly affirm and assume the goodness of God, that he possesses every attribute of

moral goodness. This renders it impossible to believe that the present is a state of rewards and punishments; that is, a state in which moral agents are dealt with precisely according to their good or ill desert. In other words, this is not a state in which God manifests his entire justice, except in our irresistible convictions, certainly not in his administration. It is easy for us to see that this state of existence must be a state of trial or probation; and that of course the manifestation of strict justice on the part of God in dispensing rewards and punishments for every act as we proceed in life, would be out of place, this being, from the very nature of a state of probation, reserved till this state of trial is ended.

We have seen that conscience points to a future state of retribution; it enforces obligation in the name of God. It always assumes that retribution is reserved till the hour of probation is ended.

3. We are aware in consciousness that our nature demands a state of moral order under the government of God as the ultimate condition of his commending himself to the universe of intelligent creatures. By moral order, I mean a state of things in which law will either be universally obeyed, or in which rewards and punishments will be in accordance with character. This state of things does not exist here. We irresistibly look forward to a future state in which moral order will be perfect.

4. If such a state is never to exist, it cannot be that God is just. Indeed, it is a contradiction to say that the Ruler of the universe is just and yet that a state of moral order will never exist under his government. An unjust God is no God. If then there be not a future state of existence, if the human soul be not immortal, there can be no God.

But should it be insisted that men are dealt with in this world according to their characters; I reply, that those who assert this know better. It is a matter of direct consciousness that we ourselves are not dealt with in this world with the severity that we deserve. And who does not know that men pass out of this world in the very act of committing the greatest crimes.

5. If the soul does not exist in a future state, our moral nature or conscience necessarily deceives us.

6. If the soul is not immortal, our moral nature is a great curse to us. It forces convictions upon us that distress and mock us.

7. If the soul is not immortal, our moral nature compels us to become atheists. For who can believe that there is a God of infinite moral perfection unless he admits that there must be a future state in which moral order will exist.

8. The moral nature of man has forced the race to assume the immortality of the soul; and this assumption has existed in despite of the fear of future punishment necessarily consequent upon this conviction. All men have known themselves to be sinners; all men have dreaded to meet God; they have feared to die, because they have assumed that "after death is the judgment." Now the fact that men have assumed and everywhere believed in the immortality of the soul, and in the justice of God, while they have known themselves to be sinners, is proof conclusive that the immortality of the soul is a dictate of our nature, and a conviction so irresistible that it cannot be disbelieved, although mankind are so interested to disbelieve it. We find in consciousness that as a general thing men disbelieve what they greatly dread; but here is a truth or fact of universal belief that exists in spite of the terror inspired by the admission.

Now what is implied in the supposition that the doctrine of immortality is not true? Why that human nature in itself is a delusion; that it forces delusions upon the whole race; and that that peculiarity of our nature that distinguishes us from the animal creation, to wit, our reason and conscience, is the greatest curse to us, inspiring us with anticipations, with hopes and fears, and pressing us with the most exciting considerations conceivable, in which, after all, there is no truth. It is plain that the assumption of immortality is natural to man and irresistible.

III. THE BIBLE ARGUMENT.

In this place it is impertinent to quote the Bible upon this subject in a course of scientific instruction, because its divine authority has not been established by us. Nevertheless, it is not out of place to notice some instances in which it is evident that the writers of the Bible assume the immortality of the soul. It has been denied that the writers especially of the Old Testament, held any such doctrine. Observe, the question now directly before us is not whether these writers were inspired; but did they believe in the immortality of the soul? Or, in other words, did they believe that the soul exists in a future state, or in a state separate from the body? Let us attend to some intimations that we find in the Old Testament.

In Deut. 18:9-12, we have a law against necromancy, that is against consulting the dead, that is departed spirits. Now from this law it is evident that the idea was at that time universal among the Jews that the soul existed after the body was dead.

Again, before the New Testament times the Jews became divided into two great sects, the Pharisees and Sadducees. This however was in their later history, that is, it was a division that existed among them at the time of the appearance of our Savior. Now it is well known that the Pharisees held the doctrine of the immortality of the soul, and that Jesus held it also. I mention not this in this place as authority, but as fact.

Again, the doctrine of Hades, or the fact that spirits existed after the death of the body and went to a place called Hades, is as evident on the face of the Old Testament Scriptures as almost any other truth found there. For example, the following texts imply it: Gen. 5:22-24, respecting the translation of Enoch. Enoch was removed from this world, it is true, in his body; but was represented as immortal, that is, as existing in a future state. Whether he continued to inhabit his fleshly body after his translation we are not informed; but from things in the New Testament we infer that his body became spiritual and immortal after his translation.

Again, in Gen. 37:35, Jacob speaks of going to his son Joseph whom he supposed to be dead; from which it is evident that he assumed that his son existed though separated from the body. See also the following passages: Gen. 15:15; 25:8; 35:29; Num. 20:24; Exod. 3:6 (compare with Mt. 22:23); Ps. 17:15; 49:15, 16, 26; Is. 26:19; Dan. 12:2; Eccl. 12:7. The phrase so often used, "gathered to his fathers," and like expressions, show that the Jewish mind was in possession of the idea of a future state of existence.

Indeed, the Old Testament in a great multitude of places, in a great variety of forms, indicates the existence of this idea in their minds; and that the immortality of the soul was assumed both by the inspired writers and by those for whose benefit they wrote. The New Testament completes the revelation. I think that no one will doubt that the New Testament writers expressly teach the immortality of the human soul, especially the immortality of the righteous.

IV. OBJECTIONS.

1. It has been objected that the soul is not naturally immortal. To this a sufficient answer has been given.

2. It has been objected that the Bible speaks of God as alone having immortality. Answer: This is meant only to assert that God is exempt from death as no man is.

3. It has been objected that the Bible declares that the wicked will be annihilated. Answer: Its language does not imply annihilation, but only ruin.

4. It has been objected, that it would be cruel to let the wicked exist and suffer eternally. Answer: This objection assumes that they do not deserve it, for admitting that they deserve it, it is certainly not cruel to treat them according to their deserts. Again, this objection assumes that there is no benevolent reason for permitting the wicked to suffer forever. Both these assumptions can be shown to be false.

Thus much for the question of immortality in this place. Again I say, I have only introduced some hints from the Bible, not as authority, but because it has been affirmed that the Jews as a nation had not anciently the idea of the immortality of the soul. An examination of the question historically will show, that the doctrine of the soul's immortality has been the doctrine of the race. It has been believed as far back as history goes, and as far as tradition throws any light upon the convictions of men.

LECTURE VIb.

INTRODUCTORY.
EVIDENCE.

BEFORE entering upon the question of the divine existence, I must remark: First, upon the importance of a correct and thorough knowledge of the laws of evidence; secondly, I must show what is evidence, and what is proof, and the difference between them; thirdly, I must inquire into the sources of evidence in a course of theological study; fourthly, must notice the kinds and degrees of evidence to be expected; fifthly, show when objections are not and when they are fatal; sixthly, how objections are to be disposed of; seventhly, on whom lies the burden of proof; and lastly; where proof or argument must begin.

I. THE IMPORTANCE OF A CORRECT AND THOROUGH KNOWLEDGE OF THE LAWS OF EVIDENCE.

1. Without a correct knowledge of this subject our speculations will be at random.

2. The ridiculous credulity of some, and the no less ridiculous incredulity of others, are owing to the ignorance or disregard of the fundamental laws of evidence. Examples: Mormonism is ridiculous credulity, founded in utter ignorance, or a disregard of the first principles of evidence in relation to the kind and degree of testimony demanded to establish anything that claims to be a revelation from God. On the other hand, every form of religious skepticism is ridiculous incredulity, founded in ignorance or the disregard of the fundamental laws of evidence, as carefully shown.

II. WHAT IS EVIDENCE AND WHAT IS PROOF, AND THE DIFFERENCE BETWEEN THEM.

1. Evidence is that which elucidates and enables the mind to apprehend truth.

2. Proof is that degree of evidence that warrants or demands belief, that does or ought to produce conviction.

3. Every degree of evidence is not proof. Every degree of light upon a subject is evidence; but that only is proof which under the circumstances can give reasonable satisfaction, while it supplies the condition of rational conviction.

III. SOURCE OF EVIDENCE IN A COURSE OF THEOLOGICAL INQUIRY.

This must depend upon the nature of the thing to be proved.

1. Consciousness may be appealed to upon questions that are within its reach, but not on other questions.

2. Sense may be appealed to on questions within the reach of sense, but not on others.

3. The existence of God may be proved, not by an appeal to the Bible as his Word, for this would be to assume his existence and his veracity, which were absurd. The existence of God must therefore be proved either *à priori*, by our irresistible convictions antecedently to all reasoning; or *à posteriori*, as an inference from his works; or in both ways.

4. The divine authority of the Bible, or of any book or thing that claims to be a revelation from God, demands some kind of evidence that none but God can give. Miracles are one of the most natural and impressive kinds; prophecy is another; the nature of the proffered revelation, its adaptedness to our nature and wants is another. These are only noticed here as kinds of evidence essential to the proof of such a question.

5. Appeals may be made to any historical fact, or thing external; or to anything internal, that is, in the Bible itself that might be reasonably expected if the revelation in question were really from God.

6. In theological inquiries, as the universe is a revelation of God, we may legitimately wander into every department of nature, science, and grace for testimony upon theological subjects.

7. The different questions must however draw their evidence from different departments of revelation: Some from the irresistible convictions of our own minds; some from his works without

us; some from his providence; others from his Word; and still others from all these together.

IV. KINDS AND DEGREES OF EVIDENCE TO BE EXPECTED.

1. In relations to kinds of evidence, I observe, no impossible or unreasonable kind is to be expected. For example, the evidence of sense is not to be demanded or expected, when the thing to be proved is not an object, or within the reach of sense. The existence of God, for example, is not given by sense, for the sense gives only the material and not the spiritual. It is absurd, therefore, for skeptics to demand the evidence of sense that God exists.

2. It is a sound rule, that the best evidence, in kind, shall be adduced that the nature of the case admits. For instance, oral testimony is not admissible where written testimony may be had to the same point. Of course, oral traditions are not to be received, where there is written history to the same point; but oral testimony is admissible in the absence of written, as then it is the best that the nature of the case admits.

3. So oral traditions may be received to establish points of antiquity in the absence of contemporary history.

4. Any book claiming to be a revelation from God, should in some way, bear his own seal, as a kind of evidence possible and demanded by the nature of the subject. The claim should be supported by evidence external and internal that make out a proof, or fulfills the conditions of rational conviction.

5. As to degree, evidence to be proof need not always amount to a demonstration, as this would be inconsistent with the nature of the case, and with a state of probation under a moral government.

6. We are not in general to expect such a degree of evidence as to preclude the possibility of cavil or evasion, and for the same reasons. On some questions we may reasonably expect to find evidence of an irresistible character; but in general it is important for us to remember that on all the important subjects of life we frequently find ourselves under the necessity of being governed simply by a preponderance of evidence—that we are in fact shut up to this often in questions of life and death. Now what we find to be

true as a matter of fact in our daily experience, we should remember may reasonably be expected on questions of theology. We shall find evidence on all practical and important subjects that ought to produce conviction, that will satisfy an upright mind; but yet on many subjects not enough to preclude all cavil or evasion. On subjects of fundamental importance, we may expect to find evidence both in kind and degree that shall put those questions beyond all reasonable doubt.

7. In regard to the divine existence, it is reasonable to expect such evidence in both kind and degree as shall gain the general assent of mankind to the fact that God exists. Such evidence certainly does exist, and this conviction has been the conviction of the race.

8. We may expect that the evidence will be more or less latent, patent, direct, inferential, incidental, full, and unanswerable, according to its relative importance in the system of divine truth.

V. WHEN OBJECTIONS ARE NOT, AND WHEN THEY ARE FATAL.

1. They are not fatal when they are not well-established by proof.

2. When the truth of the objection may consist with the truth of the proposition, that it is intended to overthrow.

3. When the truth of the affirmative proposition is conclusively established by testimony, although we may be unable to discover the consistency of the proposition with the objection. Therefore,

4. An objection is not always fatal because it is unanswerable. We may not be able to answer an objection, and yet we may have positive proof that that is true against which the objection is raised. In this case the objection is not fatal.

5. An objection is fatal, when it is an unquestionable reality, and plainly incompatible with the truth of the proposition against which it lies.

6. It is fatal when the higher probability is in its favor. That is, it is fatal in the sense that it changes the burden of proof. When the higher probability is in favor of the objection, the burden of proof then falls upon the one who would sustain the proposition against

which the objection lies. If he establishes the higher probability the onus is again changed, and the judgment ought always to decide in favor of the higher probability.

7. An objection is fatal when it is established by a higher kind or degree of evidence than the proposition to which it is opposed. For example, consciousness, sense, and reason present the highest kinds and degree of testimony. An objection fairly founded in and supported by an intuition of sense, consciousness, or reason, will set aside other testimony, because, as we have seen, knowledge thus obtained is intuitive, and more certain in its nature than that received from testimony of any other kind.

8. An objection is always fatal when it proves that the proposition against which it lies involves a palpable absurdity or contradiction.

IV. HOW OBJECTIONS ARE TO BE DISPOSED OF.

1. This depends upon their nature. If mere cavils without reason or proof, they are not properly objections, and may remain unnoticed.

2. So if they appear reasonable if they were proved, and yet are without sufficient proof, we are not gratuitously to take the burden of proof.

3. We are not bound to explain how the objection is consistent with the proposition against which it is alleged, but simply that if a fact, it may be consistent with it.

4. No objection is competent to set aside first truths, such as that a whole is equal to all its parts, that time and space exist, that every effect must have a cause, that a moral agent must be a free, self-active agent, etc. These are truths of irresistible and universal knowledge, and no testimony whatever is to be received as invalidating them.

5. No objection can set aside the direct testimony of consciousness, nor of sense or reason, where this testimony is unequivocally given.

6. Nor can any testimony set aside the unambiguous testimony of God. It is a first truth of reason that God is veracious; nobody can believe that he will lie. We necessarily assume his moral

perfection; hence the testimony of God when rightly interpreted is conclusive upon any subject, and no human being can doubt this.

There is always a fallacy in whatever is inconsistent with first or self-evident truths, the affirmation of the pure reason, the intuitions of sense or consciousness, or with the testimony of God. Certain truths we are under necessity of receiving as valid by the laws of our own intelligence. Whatever objection is made to these must involve a fallacy, and cannot be received as valid.

VII. WHERE LIES THE BURDEN OF PROOF.

1. Always on him who takes the affirmative, unless the thing affirmed is sufficiently manifest without proof.

2. The burden of proof lies with the affirmative until the evidence fairly amounts to proof in the sense of demanding belief in the absence of opposing testimony.

3. When the affirmative evidence amounts to proof in this sense, the onus is upon him who takes the negative. His business in not to prove a negative, but to counteract the proof upon the positive side of the question, to render it null, or to present so much opposing proof as will annihilate the ground of rational conviction.

4. Every kind and degree of evidence that may as well consist with the negative as with the affirmative to be proved, leaves the onus unchanged.

5. When the evidence, or argument, or an objection proves too much, as well as when it proves too little, it leaves the onus unchanged.

6. If an objection needs proof, the onus lies upon the objector.

VIII. WHERE PROOF OR ARGUMENT MUST BEGIN.

1. Proof or argument must commence where uncertainty commences; or rather where the conditions of rational belief are wanting.

2. All argument and proof take for granted such truths as need no proof, but are either axioms, self-evident truths, or such as are either admitted, or are sufficiently apparent.

LECTURE VII.

THE EXISTENCE OF GOD.

THEOLOGY is the science of God and of divine things. The knowledge of God is possible only upon condition that he reveals himself to his creatures.

I. SEVERAL WAYS IN WHICH GOD MAY REVEAL HIMSELF TO RATIONAL BEINGS.

1. Rational beings may bear his image in such a sense as irresistibly to recognize him as possessing a nature like their own. They may of necessity transfer their conception of themselves in kind, that is, so far as the attributes of their own nature are conceived, to God; and conceive of him by a necessary law as being a rational being like themselves.

In this case it is plain that he might reveal himself directly to their intuitive perceptions, so that they would recognize his existence, his presence, and the nature of his attributes: and that this revelation might be so direct as to make them certain of his existence, presence, and attributes. I do not mean by this that he could give finite creatures a comprehension of his infinity, for this were a contradiction; but I mean that the fact of his existence might be intuitively perceived, and infinity of his nature might be irresistibly affirmed.

2. This intuitive, or face to face revelation, might be made either to the moral function of the reason, that is, the conscience, or to the natural function of the reason. If made to the moral function of the reason, he would of course be known as the supreme and rightful Ruler; if to the natural function of the reason, he would be apprehended as a first cause, infinite and perfect.

3. Again, he might reveal himself in consciousness. This is an intuitive function, and reveals us to ourselves, and whatever can be properly brought within the field of our own experience. Sense must reveal to consciousness the outward world; but whatever should unify itself with our thinking, will, and feeling, may be

directly given to us in consciousness. We may be as conscious of such an embrace, and fellowship, and presence, as of our own existence.

For example, a revelation made directly to our intelligence by God might be a matter of consciousness; that is, we might not only know ourselves to be instructed, but be conscious of the source from which the instruction came. So, if peace, joy, hope, pervade our inward being, we may be aware of the source from which it comes—that is, such knowledge is possible.

4. Again, he may reveal himself to our logical faculty in such a sense, that from premises irresistibly postulated by the reason, his existence may be capable of demonstration.

5. Again, he may reveal himself in his works, through sense, in such a way as to render it natural to assume his existence; and indeed as to render it logically necessary to admit it.

6. Again, he may administer such a providence over the universe as will clearly reveal his existence to rational and reasoning beings.

7. Or again, he might reveal himself through the medium of a written revelation, in this sense: that he might produce a book in a manner and of such a character as naturally to conduct us to the conclusion that no being but God could produce such a book.

TWO REVELATIONS.

We have in fact two revelations of God; the one his works, the other his Word. His Word, the second revelation, assumes the existence and the knowledge of the first. Every attentive reader of the Bible has observed that it assumes that we already know the existence of God, and that we have an idea of his natural attributes and of his moral character; and therefore that we irresistibly assume that he is good, and that we are his subjects and ought to obey him. It never argues these questions; it does not assert them. It opens with the announcement that God made the heavens and the earth; and that he made man, and how and when he made him. Here the existence of God is taken for granted, and it is assumed that we know his existence.

Again, the second revelation, or his Word, is valid only as the first is valid, inasmuch as the second assumes the existence and validity of the first. If these assumptions have no foundation, if God has not in fact revealed himself in his works, then what we call his Word cannot be known to be his Word; and the second revelation, even if it were a revelation, would be invalid, inasmuch as its fundamental assumptions are invalid.

Again, the fundamental lessons taught in the first revelation must be learned as a condition of rationally receiving and of rightly interpreting the second. For example, being ourselves in the likeness of God, we are of ourselves a book of divine revelation. The attributes and laws of our nature are such that to understand what the Bible says of God we must to a certain extent understand ourselves, and rightly interpret the revelations which God has made to us in our nature and in the universe with which we are surrounded. Unless we recognize our moral nature, its postulates, its irresistible convictions, the law it imposes upon us, and the necessary ideas of right and wrong, we cannot understand what the Bible means. The Bible assumes that the moral law is in its essence and substance a necessary dictate of our nature; and that we have the ideas of right and wrong, and of what right and wrong in their essence are. It is only as we understand and rightly interpret the fundamental lessons given in our nature and in external nature, that we can rightly understand and interpret the Bible. Hence, they reject the Bible who fail rightly to interpret nature, understanding nature to include our own existence and attributes.

Again, they and they only fundamentally misinterpret the Bible who misinterpret nature, using the term in the sense last mentioned. I have said that the first revelation is made mostly in the laws and attributes of our own nature. From our own nature we can learn more of God, if it be rightly interpreted, then from the whole material universe. Our nature and attributes we learn directly in consciousness; hence a correct mental philosophy or psychology is indispensable to a correct interpretation of the Word of God. The first book of revelation of which we speak teaches what is generally called natural theology. It is plainly necessary that God should be revealed to us to a certain extent as the condition of any rational inquiry into the question whether the Bible be a revelation from him.

But again, suppose his existence be admitted, we must have the conviction or knowledge of his natural and moral attributes as a condition first, of settling the question whether the Bible is a revelation from him; and secondly, if it is a revelation from him, whether it is to be implicitly received. For example, unless we know his natural attributes, as his omniscience, we might suppose him mistaken in any revelation he might make, and should not feel ourselves bound, or even at liberty, to receive as unquestionable truth whatever he might say, even did we assume that it was well-informed. Again, unless we assume his omnipotence, his omnipresence, and his natural immutability, we could not be assured that he was able to do that which he wished and promised to do; or that he might not be absent on occasions when we had the promise of his aid.

Again, if we did not assume his moral attributes, we could not trust him, although we were aware of his natural attributes. His claiming to be good would not prove him to be so unless we had other evidence than merely that of his word. I do not mean to deny that we are so created as naturally and irresistibly to assume that God is to be trusted, and therefore that we do not need any other evidence than his assertion to demand our implicit confidence; but this is so just because, and only because, we are so created as necessarily to assume it. In other words, we are so created as necessarily to assume his goodness, and the existence and infinity of all his moral attributes. It is the knowledge of these obtained from the first book of revelation that makes it obligatory, or even consistent for us, to receive the second as a universally true and infallible revelation from God.

I proceed now to give that definition of God which is revealed to us in his first book of revelation; that is, to postulate what God is as known to us in the irresistible convictions of our minds, as these minds exist with out surroundings in the universe.

II. WHAT GOD IS AS KNOWN TO US IN THE IRRESISTIBLE CONVICTIONS OF OUR MINDS.

1. Such are the laws of our minds that no being can be recognized by us as the true God, a greater and better than whom can be conceived as existing or possible. When we think of God, I believe it is the universal conviction of all who have the conception of him as the self-existent, infinite God, that no greater, wiser, or better being can possibly be conceived by us; and further, that our highest and best conception of him, through just in the main, are nevertheless very inadequate; that he must, after all, be far beyond the compass of our thought, except in the sense that we affirm that he must be unlimited in all his attributes.

2. Our highest possible conception of Being is the nearest the true idea or conception of God, and just, so far as it goes.

3. Hence again, our highest possible description or definition of a Being, is the best definition of God that is possible to us. I believe it will be generally admitted that we could not conceive any being to be the true and living God of whom finiteness and imperfection were predicable. We have the idea or conception of a Being whose existence and attributes are unlimited and perfect in every respect; we define this Being to be the infinite and perfect Being; we can, we do, and must recognize this Being as God; and a greater and better we can have no idea or conception of as possible. And as I said, a finite and imperfect being we cannot conceive to be the true God. By God, then, we mean the infinite and perfect Being.

Hence, we may define God to be the infinite and perfect Being. Or, we may add to this, God the infinite and perfect First Cause. Or, we may add to this, God the infinite and perfect First Cause and Moral Governor of the universe. Or, we may vary the definition, and define him thus: God the First Cause of all finite existences, infinite and perfect. Or, God the Creator and Supreme Ruler of the universe, infinite and perfect. If we search for him by the argument *à posteriori*, and define his existence as a First Cause, we may then legitimately inquire what is implied in his being a First Cause, and thereby arrive at the attributes of infinity and perfection. Or, if we arrive at his existence through conscience as a Moral Governor, we may then properly inquire what is implied in his sustaining this relation, and thereby arrive at his infinity and perfection.

The methods of arriving at the fact of the divine existence are two: the *à priori* and the *à posteriori*. By the *à priori* method we directly assume or intuit the fact that he exists; affirm it as a first principle truth anterior to all logical reasonings. By the method *à posteriori* we reason from effect to Cause; seizing upon the events of the universe we infer his existence as a First Cause. Before entering directly upon the discussion of the question of God's existence, we must define the principle terms to be used.

III. PRINCIPAL TERMS TO BE USED IN DISCUSSION OF GOD'S EXISTENCE.

1. ABSURDITY—An absurdity is any proposition or statement that is contradictory to known truth. A proposition may be absurd when it is self-contradictory; or, it is absurd if it contradict any truth of reason, for these truths, it will be observed, are intuitive and therefore certainly known. The absurd, then, is the contradictory, that which is inconsistent either with itself or with some known truth. That may be absurd which contradicts the intuitions of sense, as well as that which contradicts the intuitions of reason; for, as we have seen, sense is an intuitive faculty and its testimony is valid. Whatever, therefore, contradicts the plain and unequivocal revelations of sense is absurd. Again, that is absurd which contradicts consciousness. Consciousness is also intuitive; all its revelations are valid; and any proposition that plainly contradicts consciousness must involve an absurdity.

2. MYSTERY—A mystery is that which is incomprehensible; that which cannot be explained by us or referred to any known law or cause. The mysterious is that which is beyond or above the comprehension of our faculties in such a sense that although it may be a fact, it is a fact inexplicable by us. The absurd is contrary to reason, the mysterious is simply beyond reason; the absurd is that which we affirm cannot be so, the mysterious is that which may be, though we may not be able to explain or even conceive how it can be. The mysterious may be true. The absurd cannot be. In theology many things are above our comprehension, as the object of our

study is the infinite. Therefore, mystery is to be expected. But in theology there can be no absurdity.

3. POWER—Power is the capacity or ability to be a cause or to produce effect.

4. CAUSE—This term is used in various senses, of which the following are the principal ones:

(1) Cause proper is an efficient; it is power in efficient or productive action. Cause implies an effect and is the efficient reason of the effect. It creates or produces. This is cause in its proper sense. Cause in this sense, as we shall soon see, must be intelligent, free, sovereign, efficient. Cause in this sense is called efficient cause.

(2) Instrumental cause. Cause in this sense is not of itself an efficient. It is not a power in itself, by only transmits an efficient power. It acts only as it is acted upon. It is neither free, sovereign, nor intelligent. Cause in this sense is an instrument and not an agent. To this category belong all the causes that are instrumentally producing the changes in the realm of unconscious matter. Cause in this sense is under the law of blind necessity. It acts as it is forced to act. I speak not now of the changes produced in the world of matter by the action of free agents, but of changes occurring under laws of necessity.

(3) Occasional cause. Occasional cause is only a motive or reason, that upon occasion of its being presented, induces a free intelligent being to act, or to become a cause in producing an effect. Cause in this sense is not an efficient. It does not compel or produce action. It is merely an instrument to act, and is as the terms denote only an occasion on which a true and proper cause acts, or a free intelligent being or power becomes a cause.

(4) Final cause. By final cause is intended the end or reason in view, and for the sake of which an intelligent being acts or becomes a cause. It is that reason that induces action, for example, the end God had in view, or the reason that induced him to cause the universe. His final end has been by necessitarian philosophers improperly called the final cause of his work of creation.

(5) Efficient cause. But to return to the consideration of efficient cause, of cause in its proper sense. Cause in this sense must be a power in itself. It is uncaused cause, as distinguished from caused or instrumental cause.

(a) It must be intelligent, as it acts upon occasion of the perception of some motive or reason for action. It must be free. It originates its own actions and is not caused to act.

(b) It must be a free agent. An agent is one who acts, and in the proper sense of the term, one who originates his own acts and is properly the author of them. A being who acts and is forced to act under a law of necessity is not capable of being a cause, in the proper sense of the term. He can be only an instrumental cause.

(c) Efficient cause must be sovereign. It must act upon occasion of some inducement, but never under a law of compulsion. It cannot be absolute in the sense of unconditional, for it acts upon occasion or condition of some perceived inducement, but it is sovereign in determining or acting in one direction or manner or another.

(d) Proper cause is not mere antecedence. It is production. Cause or causation is a mystery. There is no accounting for the self-originated acts of a free sovereign power. Such acts have no cause out of the power itself. Hence we cannot tell why an efficient cause is what it is or why the power acts as it does, and not otherwise. We may be able to tell the reasons which were the occasion of the act, but why this occasion rather than another has induced action we cannot tell. It is a mystery.

Cause and effect imply each other. Both must belong to time and neither can be eternal. A being may exist who has power to be a cause, who has never exerted that power for want of the proper occasion. The being may have existed from eternity. But from eternity he could not have been a cause. Exerting this power in an act must be an event and belong to time. But I must define event.

(6) Event. It is something that comes to pass.

(a) It may be the beginning of some existence or being.

(b) Or it may be some change in something already existent.

(c) All change is an event.

(d) Events occur in time, and cannot from their definition be eternal.

IV. SOME SELF-EVIDENT TRUTHS OF REASON.

I now proceed to postulate several self-evident truths of reason. Some of them are first truths, as they have been defined. Others are self-evident and are directly intuited by the pure reason, and must therefore be accepted as infallible truth. We have seen that cause in the most proper sense of the term, that is, efficient cause, is power in efficient action. That efficient cause must be intelligent, free, sovereign. We have also seen that an event is something that occurs, comes to pass, or take place in time. It is a change somewhere and in something. Or, it may be the beginning of something that before had no existence. As it occurs, begins, takes place, it must occur in time, and cannot be eternal. An event cannot be self-existent and eternal, for this is absurd and contradicts the true definition of an event.

1. My first postulate is that every event must have an efficient or an adequate cause. The efficient may act through or by means of an instrumental cause, or through a series of instrumental causes; but whenever there is an event, there must be a self-acting power in efficient action producing the effect immediately, or through instrumental cause or causes.

2. My second postulate is that neither cause nor effect can be eternal. This is self-evident from the definition of cause and effect. God existed from eternity with power to become a cause. When infinite wisdom called for an act of causality, he became a cause. But both the act and effect belong to time, and are not from eternity.

3. I postulate that a power acting as cause from eternity under a law of necessity is a contradiction. It is no cause if necessitated to act; it is a cause only in a secondary sense. It is therefore impossible that the material universe should have existed from eternity under a law of necessary change. In other words, it is a contradiction to say that the material universe has existed in a state of eternal change; for every change is an event, something comes to pass, and it is a contradiction to say that that which comes to

pass is eternal. That which is eternal never began to be, it is therefore no event.

4. Again, if a necessary cause were possible, a self-existent and necessary cause must be an eternal cause, and is therefore a contradiction. A being may have existed who is free and who became a cause by acting in time; but neither a self-existing and necessary, or a self-existent and free cause can be an eternal cause.

5. Again, an eternal series, therefore, of causes and events is a contradiction; because all causation and events must occur, and therefore come to pass in time.

6. Again, a self-existent being must be an unconditioned, and therefore the absolute, immutable, and infinite being. If self-existent his existence cannot be conditioned; if unconditioned in his existence he must be immutable; and if immutable he must be infinite in his being.

7. Again, a self-existent being must be absolutely perfect in every respect in which he really exists; that is, in all the attributes that inhere in his necessary existence. The term perfect is used in two senses—the relatively perfect and the absolutely perfect. By relatively perfect we mean that which is complete in its place or relations, in its adaptedness to its end. By the absolutely perfect we mean that to which nothing can be added. A self-existent being is a necessarily existent being, and exists just as it does with all its inherent properties or attributes, not one of which is capable of increase or of change; therefore, all the attributes of a self-existent being must be infinite.

8. Again, matter cannot be eternal. Whatever is eternal is self-existent. If it be eternal it never came to pass; its existence was never an event; it never had a cause. Again, whatever is self-existent is immutable. This we have seen in the last proposition above. If self-existent it exists just as it does in all its attributes from a necessity of its own nature—that is, it is eternally impossible that it should not have existed, and so existed. If the material universe existed from eternity, it existed in a quiescent state or in a state of change, from a law inherent in itself. If in a quiescent state, it was immutable in that state and could never have changed; but it does change, and therefore it is not eternal. But if it existed in a state of

change and under a law of necessary change, the cause and effect must have been eternal, which is a contradiction.

Again, if matter were self-existent, it must be eternal, absolute, immutable, infinite. That is, if it be self-existent, it is eternally existent; it must be absolute because it existence has no conditions. It must be immutable because self-existent; for self-existence is necessary existence; it must be infinite because immutable, self-existent and eternal. But matter can be neither; this is plain from the preceding proposition. Again, if matter were self-existent, the order in the material universe must have been necessary, un-changeable, and eternal. But an eternal order is a contradiction, if by order is meant order of events; for events, as we have seen, cannot be eternal.

Again, it is a contradiction because it implies an infinite series of causes and events. But this again is a contradiction; because every event and cause must belong to time, and cannot be eternal, as we have seen. Again, if matter were self-existent and eternal, neither God nor man could change it in any respect. But we know that we can change the order of events in the material universe, and produce many changes of form and order, which show clearly that the universe does not exist and act under a law of necessity. For if it did exist and act under a law of eternal necessity, then no supernatural influence could possibly exist that could vary its order. And it is also true, as we have seen, that a self-existent universe, acting under a law of eternal change, is a contradiction, as it implies an eternal series of dependent events; whereas every event, from its definition, must occur in time.

9. A cause must be a free agent exerting his power in action. A cause is a mystery only. But a cause, as we have seen, cannot be an eternal cause. A free being may be an eternal power, as is the case with God; but an eternal cause or power in an eternally-productive action, is a contradiction. It involves no contradiction to speak of a free being self-existent and eternal, who originates his own action and becomes a cause in time; but the supposition of an eternal necessity in nature is not a mystery, it is a contradiction, as in that case cause and effect must have been eternal.

10. Again, as we have seen, a cause must be a free agent. We have seen that an agent is an actor. An agent exerting his power in producing actions, is a free, and hence a proper cause. Again, I am conscious of being a free cause. I am a moral agent and therefore free; I act myself in producing effects. In these actions I am cause; I know myself to be a cause, and a free cause, by being directly conscious of it. Hence I know that I am a supernatural being; in the actions of my will I am not subject to the law of cause and effect; the volitions of my will are causes. Of this I am conscious.

11. Again, we know that matter is not in any case a cause, in the highest sense of the term. It may transmit an influence which it receives; but all that we can know is, that in nature events succeed each other, under a law of necessity. The power cannot reside in matter itself; matter can be only an instrumental cause. An influence may be transmitted from the great First Cause through this chain of material causes, but we have seen that proper causes must be intelligent and free.

But in consciousness we know ourselves as proper causes; that the power by which we become cause is our own; and that we exert it at discretion, and under a law, not of necessity, but of moral responsibility. No intuitive faculty of ours can give us any other cause than that of free power in action; and this cause is directly given in consciousness.

V. ARGUMENT FOR THE EXISTENCE OF GOD.

The proposition to be proved is the existence of God, first as a First Cause of all finite existences. The method of proof in this case must be *à posteriori*. But although the method must be *à posteriori*, it must have an *à priori* foundation; in other words, we must use two postulates of the reason as the foundation of our argument. The method, therefore, in this case, although called *à posteriori*, is strictly a combination of the *à priori* and *à posteriori*.

Foundation postulate: (1) Every event must have a cause. (2) An eternal series of dependent events is a contradiction. Syllogism— major premise: A series of dependent events implies a First Cause. Minor premise: The universe is a series of dependent events. Conclusion: There must be a First Cause.

1. Proposition: The First Cause must be infinite and perfect. Syllogism—major premise: Whatever is self-existent must be immutable, infinite, and perfect in all its attributes. This we have seen among the postulates of the pure reason. Minor premise: The First Cause must be self-existent, and therefore immutable, infinite, and perfect in all its attributes. Conclusion: God is, and is the First Cause, and therefore infinite and perfect.

2. Proposition: A first cause must be a free cause. Syllogism—major premise: A first cause is an uncaused cause. Minor premise: None but a free cause can be uncaused. Conclusion: Therefore, the first cause must be free.

VI. ARGUMENT FOR THE EXISTENCE OF GOD AS MORAL GOVERNOR.

This, as in proving the existence of God as a First Cause, is to prove his existence in a certain relation. Having proved his existence in certain relations, it is then proper to inquire what attributes are implied as belonging to his nature, and his character. These may be ascertained by an intuitive perception of what is implied in his existence in these relations.

1. God is a moral governor, infinite and perfect. In a former lecture the existence of conscience, as revealed in consciousness, came under consideration. This faculty, as we there saw, and as we are at present aware in consciousness, postulates an authoritative rule of moral action with sanctions. That is, this faculty affirms our obligation to be universally benevolent, and affirms this obligation in the name of God as the moral governor to whom we affirm our accountability. The moral nature of conscience, or in other words the reason in its moral application, is so related to God that it necessarily knows and assumes his existence. Within ourselves we are conscious of subjective moral law in the form of an authoritative rule of action. We are conscious of being amenable to an Author of this law, whom we cannot avoid conceiving to be the Author of our nature. We cannot resist the assumption that this Being has a claim upon our love and obedience; and it is to him that we necessarily regard ourselves as being amenable. In this our moral nature directly assumes and *à priori* intuits his existence as

the Author of our nature, and of the law within us which we necessarily impose upon ourselves.

2. Again, in postulating obligation to universally submit to, obey, and trust him, our conscience or moral nature irresistibly assumes his infinity and perfection, both natural and moral. Did we not necessarily conceive of him as naturally perfect, we might suppose that he might err, and therefore as not worthy of universal confidence and obedience, however well he might intend. If we did not assume his moral infinity and perfection, we could not conceive ourselves under universal obligation to obey, submit to, and trust him. But our conscience or moral nature does unequivocally affirm our obligation to obey him implicitly and universally, to trust him implicitly and universally, and universally to submit to all his dealings. This affirmation being an ultimate fact of consciousness, is conclusive of his existence and perfections.

3. Again, we are aware in consciousness that conscience as truly postulates and assumes the existence of God as consciousness does our own existence. In other words, we are directly conscious of our own existence, and we are directly conscious that conscience assumes the existence of God. The one of these functions is as reliable as the other; they are both intuitive functions. Conscience gives the existence of God as a direct intuition or assumption in postulating our obligation to love and trust him; consciousness gives our own existence directly in our internal exercises. So that in postulating the existence of God and my obligation to him by my conscience, I am aware of my own existence in this assumption of my conscience; and thus these two existences, my own and the existence of God, are simultaneously revealed to me—my own directly by consciousness and God's directly by my conscience or moral nature. Both existences are thus revealed to me in consciousness; my own directly by consciousness, and God's indirectly through my conscience.

It is in this way, beyond all doubt, that mankind in general first come to the knowledge of the existence of God. It is not by reasoning, but by the *à priori* intuitions of conscience. He is not first known as a First Cause by the reason and logical faculty cooperating in the demonstration. As a First Cause he is known *à posteriori*; as a Moral Governor *à priori*. And indeed, it is impossible that as a Moral Governor he should be known in any other way. As Moral Governor he reveals himself to moral agents by revealing to their intuitive perceptions their obligation to him. Their obligation to him is not an inference from his existence and their relations to him as Creator. For were it admitted that he existed and that he were our Creator, it would not follow that we are under obligation to obey him, unless he be worthy of obedience. But how are we to learn that he is worthy of obedience? This we cannot get at by reasoning as a condition of our moral obligation to obey him.

We know ourselves to have been moral agents antecedent to all reasoning on the subject of the character of God. Ever moral agent knows that he assumed from the very beginning of his moral agency his obligation to obey God, and his amendability to him, anterior to all reasoning as it respects the moral character of God, or even his existence. God's existence, therefore, and moral character, are directly and intuitively revealed to the moral nature of every moral agent; and it is this intuitive revelation of his existence and character that is the condition of moral obligation to him. Now who does not know that he had the ideas of right and wrong, of moral obligation, of praise or blame-worthiness, before he had ever reasoned either concerning the existence or the attributes of God.

The existence of God, then, as a Moral Governor, is a fact revealed in the conscience, and consequently consciousness, of every moral agent. So true is this that men find it impossible to rid themselves of the idea of his existence in affirming their obligation and amendability to him.

4. Again, no moral agent under the pressure of conscience or standing in the presence of affirmed obligation, ever did or can doubt the existence of God and his amendability to him. It is an absurdity and a contradiction to say that, in the presence of postulated obligation and accountability to God by the conscience, the existence of God should really be doubted.

5. Again, the existence of God is only doubted when by improper methods an attempt is made to prove that he exists; or

under the influence of some temptation that diverts the attention for the time being from the authoritative voice of God.

6. Again, the idea of future retribution as it lies in the universal conscience is an assumption of the existence of God. We necessarily conceive of God as just; all sinners are necessarily aware that they have disobeyed him. Now the conception of his moral perfection, and the consciousness that we have disobeyed him, lead to the irresistible assumption of the fact of a future retribution. This assumption of course includes the assumption of God's existence.

7. Again, it is generally agreed that man has a religious nature, that is, a nature that demands religion. Even atheists admit that man is by nature a superstitious being, which implies that by nature they assume the existence of God, or moral obligation, etc. Now, whether our nature be assumed to be a religious nature or a superstitious nature, it really amounts to the same thing. We have a nature that craves or demands the existence of God, that affirms his existence and our amendability to him. Call this a natural superstition, or a natural assumption, that God exists and claims our obedience—call it what you will, the fact remains that by nature we assume and know the existence of God; and that this assumption is natural, not as a logical deduction, but as an intuitive knowledge. Again, if conscience did not give God as an irresistible conviction, or an intuitive knowledge, guilt and selfishness would reject the fact. But the fact cannot be rejected just because the knowledge is intuitive.

8. Again, moral agency is an ultimate fact of consciousness; moral agency implies moral law and accountability. Accountability implies a Moral Ruler or Governor. Moral government implies moral law; moral law is necessarily perfect and implies a perfect Moral Ruler; and a perfect Moral Ruler must be infinite. Therefore, the moral argument gives God as the infinite and perfect Moral Governor of the universe.

LECTURE VIII.

THE EXISTENCE OF GOD
(CONTINUED).

I. ARGUMENT FROM FINAL CAUSES; *OR, as it is better expressed,* FROM APPARENT DESIGN.

1. SYLLOGISM—Major premise: Design implies a designing mind. Minor premise: The universe exhibits conclusive proof of design. Conclusion: Therefore the universe is the product of competent designing mind.

2. Second syllogism—Major premise: The mind that designed and created the universe is the first cause. Minor premise: But the first cause must be a self-existent, and therefore, as we have seen, immutable, infinite, and perfect being. Conclusion: Therefore God exists, the infinite and perfect First Cause.

The minor premise of the first of the above syllogisms I have not attempted to prove. If anyone calls in question the fact that the universe presents innumerable and conclusive evidences of benevolent design, this is not the place to enlarge upon a subject so extensive. So many treatises have been written upon this subject, so much has been said in respect to the indubitable evidences of design in the construction and working of the universe, that it were a work of supererogation in this connection to attempt to prove it. Suffice it to say in a word, that the revelations of science and [sic.] continually pouring floods of additional light upon this question, insomuch that even the rocks speak out and bear their testimony that they were created by a designing mind.

II. FACTS AND SELF-EVIDENT TRUTHS.

1. We have seen that in consciousness we know ourselves to exist; and that we know the existence of that which is not ourselves. I say, we know this in consciousness. It is certain that the very conception of self as self implies also the conception of that which is not self. Should it be said that we are not directly conscious of that which is not self, I answer, that this may be true

of the material creation; that is, it may be true and indeed must be true that sense gives the material not self; but it should be remembered that sense is an intuitive faculty and gives its object by a direct beholding of it, just as consciousness gives its object by a direct beholding. The thing of which we are conscious is that we directly behold the not self. It is not so much a matter of consciousness that this beholding is by the faculty of sense; for I am just as conscious of seeing or directly knowing the outward world as I am the inward world. I am just as conscious of knowing the not self as I am of knowing the self. I am conscious of this knowledge, and am just as certain of the existence of the one as of the other. So far as certainty is concerned, therefore, it amounts to the same thing whether it is obtained by one faculty of intuition or the other. The knowledge is intuitive and certain, of this knowledge I am conscious; and whether in strict propriety of speech I am conscious directly of the existence of the not self, or of the outward world, or whether on the other hand, I am conscious of knowing it through the medium of sense, is immaterial so far as the fact of this knowledge is concerned.

But here it should be said, that although it is true in strict propriety of speech that we become conscious of the existence of the outward world only through the intuitions of sense, this is not true in respect to the existence of other beings of whose existence we are directly conscious. In another place I shall endeavor to show that we are directly conscious of the existence of God, and this certainly is not given us through sense. But here I wish to be particularly understood to say, that so far as certainty is concerned, it matters not at all through which of the intuitive functions of the intellect we get at truth. If it be by intuition, the certainty cannot be called in question without denying the validity of all knowledge. If one intuitive function of the intellect may deceive us, in other words, if we are not certain of what we directly behold in consciousness, sense, or reason, if each of these faculties is not to be trusted, neither of them is to be. We can no more doubt the validity of the testimony of one than the other. We are certain of that which we intuit; and if we are not, there is no distinguishing the intuitions of one faculty from another in such a way as to know which is to be trusted. They are all alike veracious, or all alike untrustworthy.

2. There is a material nature.

3. There is an order in this nature.

4. First self-evident truth: This nature and this order in nature has a cause out of itself, or it is self-existent and has the law of its order written within itself. If it is self-existent and has the law of its order written within itself, then it is by a necessity of its own nature eternally just as it is and has been, and therefore immutable, eternal, and infinite.

This we have seen in former propositions, and it needs not to be enlarged upon.

5. Second self-evident truth: Matter cannot be infinite; for it must have a form, and form implies limitation, and therefore finiteness. To speak of matter as having no form is a contradiction. To speak of form as being infinite is also a contradiction. Again, it cannot be infinite, for it is made up of finite parts or particles, and no number of units or finites can ever make an infinite.

Again, it has been shown that if matter is self-existent it must be eternal, infinite, immutable. But it cannot be immutable because we ourselves know that we can introduce many changes in it. That is, if the universe of matter is self-existent and has the law of all its changes inherent in itself, then there is no power that can vary in the least degree these changes; for the law of these changes, if matter be self-existent, must be absolutely omnipotent. In other words, if matter exists and changes under a law of necessity, it is a contradiction to say that any power in the universe, or any conceivable power, can vary the order of these changes.

But as I said, we ourselves know that we change this order, and we know that those around us introduce innumerable variations in the order of changes going on in the material universe around about us.

Dr. Chalmers and others have admitted that without damage to the theistic argument, we may admit that matter is self-existent and therefore eternal. "For," he says, "we must not necessarily suppose the existence of God to account for the collocation of matter." But I

104

cannot consent to this, for the reason, that if matter does eternally exist, necessity must be an attribute of its nature, and in every respect in which it does exist it exists by this necessity, and consequently it is necessarily immutable. That is, no change can ever be introduced into it except under the action of its own inherent necessary laws; and these laws must, to all intents and purposes, be omnipotent; that is, they must have power to resist any conceivable power that might set upon them. To suppose the contrary were to deny the self-existence and therefore the necessary existence of matter. If God did not create the materials out of which the universe is formed, if those materials do in fact exist independent of him, that is, if they are self-existent, the supposition that God could form the material universe and locate matter as we find it located out of self-existent materials, is an absurdity.

In the light of the above,

III. THE FOLLOWING POSITIONS ARE MANIFEST:

1. A self-existent material universe, having an eternal and necessary order of development, is first an absurdity.

2. It contradicts consciousness, for we are aware ourselves of acting upon it and changing the order of its development, which could not be were it self-existent and under a law of necessary development.

3. It follows that material nature and its order commenced in time. We have seen that order must be made up of succeeding events, for order can belong to nothing else than changes, but changes must occur in time. Should it be said, that nature itself may have been eternal, and its changes have commenced in time; I answer, this is a contradiction, if this nature has the law of its development or changes in itself. If this law is in itself, then these changes must have been coeval with the existence of that in which this law resides. But eternal changes are a contradiction; and an eternal nature having a law of change in itself is a contradiction, because no eternal changes, and consequently no eternal law of change, can possibly exist.

4. The material universe must have had a cause out of and superior to itself; its existence and changes cannot otherwise by

any possibility be accounted for. Indeed, it is a contradiction to affirm the existence of nature, and the order of its changes, except upon the admission that it had a cause out of itself.

5. The cause of the material universe must be a self-existent, and therefore an infinite Being. We have seen that a necessary cause is a contradiction; for a self-existent necessary cause must be an eternal cause, or imply eternal acts of causation; for be it remembered that cause is power in producing action. I say, therefore, that the cause of the material universe must be a self-existent, and therefore a necessarily existent, immutable, infinite Being.

6. Again, this Being must be a free and intelligent Being. No being can be free in the proper sense of freedom who is not intelligent; for free will acts only upon conditions of perceived reasons for action; therefore freedom always implies intelligence.

7. Again, this First Cause must be naturally perfect; that is, every attribute which he possesses must be infinite, and therefore perfect in the highest sense of perfection.

8. Again, we have seen in a former lecture that the ideas of the finite and the infinite are contrasts, always exist together in the mind, and that neither can be held without the other. The same we have seen to be true of the ideas of the perfect and the imperfect, and also of the conditioned and the unconditioned, of succession and time, of body and space. One of these ideas, then, implies the other; and where one is the other must be. But does the fact of the existence of the finite imply the existence of the infinite; the existence of the imperfect that of the perfect; the existence of the conditioned that of the unconditioned? I answer, yes.

(1) Because no finite being is self-existent. Every finite existence, therefore, must have begun to be in time, must have had a cause; and as an infinite series of causes and effects is a contradiction, there must be a First Cause.

(2) An imperfect being cannot be a self-existent being; for whatever is self-existent, we have seen, must be infinite, and therefore every attribute which a self-existent being possesses must be perfect in the highest conceivable sense, since, being infinite, nothing can be conceived to be wanting. If then, there be an

imperfect being, it must be a dependent being; but this implies the existence of a First Cause, infinite and perfect.

(3) The same is true of a conditioned being. The very conception of a conditioned being is that of a dependent being, that is, dependent for existence. Such a being, therefore, cannot be self-existent. But if not self-existent, it must have been created; and there must have been a First Cause, which must be self-existent and unconditioned.

IV. PROPOSITIONS, in the light of the foregoing.

1. First proposition: If any event ever occurred, an infinite and perfect God exists. Syllogism: Major premise: We have seen that events imply the existence of a First Cause. Minor premise: We have seen also that a First Cause must be self-existent and therefore infinite and perfect. Conclusion: Therefore if any event exists, God exists, the infinite and perfect.

2. Second proposition: If any consciousness exists, God exists, the infinite and perfect. Syllogism: Major premise: Consciousness must be either an eternal and infinite, or a finite consciousness. If an infinite consciousness, then it must be the consciousness of God, and God exists; if finite consciousness, it is an event. Minor premise: But the existence of any event, as we have seen, implies the existence of an infinite and perfect Cause. Conclusion: Therefore if any consciousness exists, God the infinite and perfect exists.

3. Third proposition: If any doubt of the existence of God exists, God must exist. Syllogism: Major premise: The existence of doubt is an event. Minor premise: The existence of any event, as we have seen, implies the existence of an infinite First Cause. Conclusion: Therefore, if any doubt exists of God's existence, God the infinite and perfect must exist.

4. Fourth proposition: If God's existence be denied, his existence must be a fact. Syllogism: Major premise: The denial of the existence of God must be an event. Minor premise: The existence of any event implies the existence of an infinite and perfect First Cause. Conclusion: Therefore, if God's existence was ever denied, his existence must be a fact.

5. Fifth proposition: If atheists exist, God exists. Syllogism: Major premise: the existence of an atheist is an event. Minor premise: The existence of any event implies the divine existence. Conclusion: Therefore, if there be an atheist in existence, God the infinite and perfect exists.

V. STATING THE SUBSTANCE OF THE ABOVE PROPOSITIONS IN ANOTHER FORM.

1. If any event ever occurred, an infinite, free, and perfect Being must exist; showing, if any event ever occurred it must have been finite, dependent, and in time. Finite, because an infinite event is an absurdity; dependent, because whatever is not infinite is not necessary and therefore cannot be independent. That is, it must be dependent in time, because an event is an occurrence, a something that comes to pass, begins to be. An eternal event is impossible and a contradiction; it must, therefore, occur in time.

2. If anything finite, dependent, and commencing in time exists, it must have had a cause out of and superior to itself. This we have abundantly seen. Therefore, if anything finite, dependent, commencing in time, exists there must be a First Cause; and this Cause must be a self-existent, eternal and necessary Being; that is, his existence must be necessary, or the ground of his existence is in himself. But as a Cause, he must be free. We have seen that a necessary Cause must be an eternal Cause, and that an eternal Cause implies eternal events, which is a contradiction. A First Cause, then, must be a free, intelligent Cause; hence if any event ever occurred, there must be an infinite, free, and perfect Being existing as a First Cause.

But of this First Cause let me further say: We have seen that a First Cause must be a self-existent Being, consequently that he must be immutable in all his attributes; he must therefore be infinite in all his attributes; and an absolutely perfect Being must be perfect in all the attributes which he possesses.

3. Again, we have seen that the existence of atheism as an event implies the divine existence.

4. Again, if the possibility and reality of theism should be denied, the denial itself would be an event and imply the existence of God.

5. From the foregoing propositions, it follows, that if the universe of creatures is all matter, God must exist as the infinite and perfect First Cause.

6. Again, if the universe of creatures is all mind, as the Idealists maintain, God must exist as the First Cause. The same is true if the universe is only thought, as the extreme school of Idealists maintain. The existence of thought is an event, and really implies the existence of an infinite and perfect First Cause.

7. But further, it has been laid down as a self-evident pro-position, that whatever is self-existent is infinite. Of matter it should also be said that it cannot be infinite, for since one of its essential properties is form, and whatever has form cannot be infinite, it must therefore be finite and dependent, and imply the existence of a First Cause out of and above itself; which First Cause is self-existent, infinite, and perfect.

8. Again, our own minds we know to be limited or finite. Our conscious existence implies the existence of God.

9. Again, from what has been said it follows, that whether the universe is all matter, or all mind, or only thought, or whether all this matter, mind, and thought exist, God's existence is equally implied as the infinite and perfect First Cause.

10. Again, knowing ourselves to exist, the nonexistence of God is inconceivable; therefore nihilism is a contradiction and an impossible conception. Suppose any one would say, that he could conceive that nihilism should be true, in the assertion he contradicts himself. He says, I can conceive that there is no existence; but who has this conception? And what is the conception itself? The very existence of the conception shows the absurdity of the statement; and that he who affirms that it is possible that nothing does in fact exist contradicts himself; no such conception is conceivable.

VI. ARGUMENT FROM CONSCIOUSNESS OF THE EXISTENCE OF GOD.

1. Man is capable of being directly taught of God; this cannot be rationally denied. We are conscious of being spirit, and we necessarily conceive of him as spirit. If any one denies that God as a Spirit can instruct our spirits by a direct communication with us, the burden of proof is certainly on him.

2. Again, man is capable of being conscious that he is taught of God. The prophets were so; and every spiritual mind has this consciousness at times. If it be asked how the prophets knew that they were directly inspired of God, I cannot tell; and perhaps they could not tell how God taught them. But they were distinctly conscious that it was God, and no other than God, that taught them. If it should be objected, as it may be, that they may have been deceived, that the false prophets certainly were deceived and therefore all prophets may have been; I answer, it is true that men may be deceived, as in a dream they may think themselves awake; nevertheless, when they are awake they are aware of it. So if a false prophet may have been deceived, it does not follow that the true prophets were not sure that they were not deceived. If God can directly inspire a man, he can certainly make him aware that he is not deceived; else how could an honest man ever affirm himself to be inspired by God? But if God can directly and personally teach the human mind, and we can be personally aware of it; then we can be conscious of the existence of God in the fact that he personally enlightens and instructs us.

3. But again, man is capable of communion, and sympathy, and moral union with God. If anyone denies this, the burden of proof is upon him. Our necessary conception of God is that he is a mind as we are; that he has intellect, sensibility, and will, as we have. We necessarily conceive ourselves as being in his image. Now this necessary conception which we have of God must be substantially the time [sic.] conception. To deny it were to call in question our fundamental and irresistible convictions; or in other words, to deny a first truth of reason.

If, then, man is in the image of God, he must be capable of knowing him, of sympathizing with him, and of moral union with him, agreeing with him in design or motive, living for the same end for which he lives. And it is plain that this sympathy may be a sympathy with his views, and therefore intellectual; with his choice, and therefore moral; and with his feelings, and therefore belonging to the sensibility. Thus our whole mind is capable of this communion, and union, and sympathy with God.

4. Again, if we have this communion, and sympathy, and union, we must be conscious of it.

5. Again, millions of the wisest and best of human beings have had this consciousness for years, have avowed this consciousness, have lived in accordance with the existence of such a consciousness. Now, the existence of this consciousness is to the individual a certain knowledge of the existence of God; he is conscious of the existence of God in his personal knowledge of him, communion and sympathy with him. By this I do not mean that he is conscious of his infinity; but he is conscious that he has union with the divine mind, with one whom he certainly regards as infinite and perfect. To the individual, the existence of God is a fact in consciousness.

6. Again, the testimony of those who have this consciousness is valid. They are competent witnesses; they are credible witnesses. Myriads of them in every way, in life and death, give evidence of entire sincerity, and also of being intelligent in their affirmations. Now this testimony is good in its kind; for if one cannot testify to that of which he is conscious, of what can he testify? For this is a certain form of knowledge. The testimony, then, of witnesses who give the highest evidence of sincerity and of virtue in their life and death that can be given, is valid testimony.

To this, it may be, and HAS BEEN **OBJECTED, FIRST,** that multitudes have evidently been deceived. To this I answer: Evidently been deceived? How has this deception been evident? Has it appeared in their lives or temper? Or, have they testified to contradictions and abnormalities? The objection assumes that there was evidence that they were deceived. Now I admit that many have been deceived, and have given evidence that they were deceived, but this does not begin to prove that all have been deceived. Of many it cannot be said that they have evidently been deceived; for there is no evidence that they were deceived, but the highest evidence that they were not deceived. The fact that many have been deceived does not prove by any means that others may not know that they are not deceived; any more than that a man's supposing himself to be awake when he is asleep proves that he cannot know when he is awake.

OBJECTION SECOND: This argument from consciousness may be, and is, plead by the Spiritists. They affirm that they are conscious of direct communion with spirits. To this I answer (1) That the cases are not parallel. Those who are conscious of communion with God are aware of this communion in its directly transforming influence in giving to them a new inward experience, or a new inward spiritual life, filling them with love, joy, and peace, and adorning views of his attributes and character; of the purifying and elevating influence of this communion. In short, they are not merely aware of its being communion with a spirit, but with a Divine Spirit; and that this communion is to them a new life, spiritual, heavenly; and that it influences the will, the intellect, and the sensibility, and is transforming in its influence, covering the whole of our inward experience and developing itself in a holy life. Now nothing like this is so much as affirmed by the Spiritualists. Most of their affirmations are manifestly inferences which they draw from material facts. They hear a rapping, and infer that it is a spirit. But this is no consciousness; they are only conscious of hearing raps. Again, they profess to hear words; to be taught to write involuntarily, or without knowing what they write; to be taught to speak in an unknown tongue, without knowing what they speak; and sometimes to speak impromptu, not from themselves, but from spirits with them.

Now who does not see that all this is inference? Suppose all the facts which they allege really exist; the testimony is not in point. How do they know that it is a spirit that moves their hand? And that it is such or such a spirit? How do they know that it is a spirit that produces these effects? Are they directly conscious of this spirit within themselves in such a sense as Christians are conscious of communion with God? I am not aware that Spiritists make any such pretensions. But if they do, do they give as high evidence of sincerity, intelligence, and honesty, as spiritual and heavenly minded Christians do? Now I must say that I do not believe that any such testimony in favor of Spiritism exists, or ever did exist.

But (2), If this kind of testimony does in fact exist, which is really the testimony of consciousness, of course it is to be received. The testimony of consciousness is conclusive, and not to be disposed of by such an objection as this. If Spiritists can actually give us the testimony of consciousness that they have had communion with spirits, and know them—if they are directly conscious of this, it must be true. No one surely can affirm that no such communion is possible; but do they have such communion? Do they give so high evidence to others that they have this communion, that their testimony ought to be received by them? I do not believe that any such testimony exists among them.

Again, while I admit that the testimony of consciousness with regard to communion with finite spirits might be valid, yet I do not admit that it could be valid in the same sense in which the testimony of conscious communion with God can be valid. If God communes with us and we with him, he must be interested to make us fully aware of it. He is able to make us fully aware of it, and to render it impossible that we should be deceived; and such in fact has been the consciousness of the inspired writers and of spiritual Christians in all ages. They really no more doubt their communion with God than they doubt their own existence. If you ask them how they know it, they cannot tell how, anymore than they can tell how they can see an object when their eyes are open upon it; nor any more than they can tell how they are conscious of their own existence. But they can tell you that this communion is to them an indubitable reality; that while it exists it cannot be doubted; and that it is only when it has passed away and cannot be renewed in consciousness, that it is possible to doubt it.

7. Again, in the course of theological inquiries it will be seen that the testimony of consciousness is conclusive upon many theological questions. I have been astonished that so little importance seemed to be attached by Christians, and Christian writers, to this form of testimony. I know that it has been objected that it will not be received by skeptics. But why should it not? Skeptics can resist the evidence of miracles, can deny the evidence of their

sense, can call in question first truths of reason; but after all they possess minds, and with all their denials it is impossible for them to get rid of the deep conviction that such a testimony ought to be received. I ask, why should not skeptics receive the oral and written testimony of millions of spiritual minds that affirm that they know God by a direct personal knowledge and intercourse with him; that they are aware of communion with him, of being taught by him, of being led, sustained, and saved from sin by him? They have testified that their communion with him has resulted in a radical change of the great end of their being; that it has resulted in the permanent reformation of their lives; that they have for years kept up habitually and more or less constantly this communion with him, the result of which has been evident to all that knew them. Thus they have lived on the comforts of this intercourse with God; thus they have been sustained in holy living and triumphing over the trials of life; and thus they have died, testifying in life and death that God is, that they know him, have communion with him, and walk with him.

Now why should not this testimony be received on this subject? They surely are competent witnesses in the sense that they know what they say and whereof they affirm. They are also credible witnesses; for they give every evidence in life and in death of entire honesty. Again, they are innumerable, and are uniform in their testimony and agree together. No fact then was ever established by so good and so much testimony from human beings as this. Why, then, should infidels not receive it? To say that individuals have been deceived is nothing to the purpose; for in cases where individuals have been deceived, it is admitted that they have given evidence of being deceived. If this were not so, then there is no ground for saying that any ever were deceived. But what shall we say of those who have given evidence of being deceived? The fact that others have been deceived on a question of consciousness, in other words, have misinterpreted the facts of consciousness, or have never had in fact any such consciousness, is no ground for the contention that all have been deceived.

In consciousness I know God through my sensibility, and not through my intelligence merely. With my eyes shut I can recognize the presence of heat. I never saw heat. But I know it in feeling. God sheds his love, that is, himself, abroad in my sensibility. I know that this is God's love, and yet that it is in my heart. I feel it and cannot but know it is God. I cannot tell how I know it; the fact I know. To deny this is to shut us up to speculation, and shut us out from all really transforming knowledge of God. The intuitive function, sense, gets all its intuitions through the sensibility. Sense is spiritual, although the organs of sense are material. In consciousness I seem to have a sense that is related to God. Material objects are revealed to me in and through sensation. I do no infer the existence of the material from sensation, but through sensation I directly behold the material. So in the warmth and light and love and peace and joy of our inward experience I directly and irresistibly recognize God. I feel after God and find him, and I know that I feel and find God. If we can know our organism, or the not me in consciousness, surely we may know God in consciousness. I am conscious of God. The how I do not know. This, like all other knowledge is a mystery as to the how. (This paragraph added later, in different hand writing, perhaps when he was old).

VII. METHOD OF THE NATURAL REASON.

We have seen that the moral function of the reason, conscience, directly assumes the existence of God as Moral Governor. But does the natural reason, or the function of the reason applied to natural objects and truths, as distinguished from moral objects and truths, necessarily assume and affirm the existence of God? I answer, Yes. Our own existence is a fact, an ultimate fact of consciousness. The existence of the human race is itself a fact of consciousness. This fact of our own conscious existence is the platform on which we stand. This fact is assumed; and it is impossible for us to forget it or not to assume it. Now the human reason, assuming as it does its own existence, directly affirms the existence of God as its logical antecedent, or more strictly as the condition of its existence. God's existence it knows to be implied in the fact of its own existence.

The human reason, therefore, necessarily assumes the existence of God as being implied in its own existence. The fact of its own existence and the existence of God are both intuitively and necessarily affirmed, self-existence in reason implying the existence of God. Therefore, knowing as we do, by an absolute knowledge, that we ourselves exist, it is really a necessary and universal assumption of reason that God exists; and in this sense the existence of God is a first truth of reason, a truth of universal and necessary assumption.

VIII. SUMMARY REMARKS.

Where, then, do we find ourselves at the present stage of our inquiries on the question of the divine existence?

1. His existence has been demonstrated by the argument *à posteriori*, reasoning from effect to cause.

2. The reality of his existence has been shown to be an *à priori* knowledge of conscience.

3. The reality of his existence has also been shown to be a necessary assumption of the reason, implied in its existence. That man being conscious of his own existence, and reason necessarily assuming its own existence, affirms the existence of God directly as the logical condition of its own existence.

4. It has been shown that the fact of his existence is, in multitudes of cases, a truth or a fact of direct and personal consciousness.

5. It has been shown that as certain as any fact or event ever existed, whatever that fact or event might be, God exists. If there ever was any event, God exists. If there ever was a phenomenon, God exists. If there ever was an act, or a thought, or a doubt in existence, God exists. If this is not proof sufficient and conclusive, then it is impossible to prove anything. It has been said, and strangely enough, that the existence of God could not be proved. But we have seen the contrary. Indeed, it is easy to prove the existence of God in so many ways and by such an accumulation of evidence, that to deny his existence is simply ridiculous.

6. The testimony from consciousness or experience is, after all, that which will most affect and best satisfy a certain class of skeptics, matter of fact minds. There are certain important though unrecognized distinctions between:

(1) How we know and how to prove to others certain truths, for example, the existence of God. We know by intuition, conscious experience. We prove by demonstration, and by our own testimony. We know *à priori*, we prove *à posteriori*.

(2) We know the truths given by reason, consciousness, and sense, by intuition. We prove the truths of reason by a perspicuous statement, of consciousness and sense, either by our own testimony or by appeals to the consciousness and sense of those to be convinced.

(3) We know many things that we cannot prove, that is, our personal identity, our moral liberty or freedom.

(4) He who insists upon proving everything, can prove nothing.

(5) Truths that we know by intuition, either of reason, consciousness, or sense, we cannot prove to ourselves, because there is no truth more certainly known from which to reason.

LECTURE IX.

THE NATURAL ATTRIBUTES OF GOD.

HAVING, as we suppose, sufficiently discussed the question of the divine existence, the next question for discussion in the natural order of our course is, the natural attributes of God. And the first inquiry is into the method by which we are to ascertain what these attributes are.

We have ascertained first, that God is the First Cause of all finite existences; and secondly, that he is infinite and perfect in his natural attributes. The question, then, of his natural attributes must be settled by a consideration of what must be implied in his being the infinite and perfect First Cause of all finite existences. The question of his moral attributes must be arrived at more particularly through the medium of conscience, or the moral function of the reason. It will be observed that the inquiry is rational in the sense, not that it belongs to the department of natural theology, but that it is particularly that function of the intellect which we denominate the reason, by the use of which we are to ascertain the kind and extent of the natural attributes of God.

I. WHAT IS A NATURAL ATTRIBUTE?

But first, I must define a natural attribute. An attribute is a permanent quality of a thing. This is its generic definition. It is that which is predicable of a thing as essential to its nature. The natural attributes of God are those permanent qualities which belong to his nature; those qualities without which he would not be God.

Again, I remark that the existence of these qualities in God is indicated in the things that he has made. But the infinity of these attributes is not demonstrated in the works of creation, for nothing which has been created is infinite. But the infinity of his attributes is nevertheless irresistibly implied, as we shall see, in his being a First Cause.

For example, we do not logically infer the omnipotence, the omniscience, or the absolute ubiquity of God from his works; for we cannot know that it required absolute omnipotence to create finite works; nor his ubiquity from his presence throughout the material universe; nor his omniscience from his possessing sufficient knowledge to create the universe. Intelligence, power, extension, must be implied in his being the Cause of the universe. But as a Cause he cannot be infinite, that is, he never has exerted the whole of infinity in producing action. In other words, an infinite Cause would imply an infinite effect, which is impossible and a contradiction.

We have seen that cause is power in producing action. Now a being may be infinite without ever exerting the whole of his infinite power in an act of causality; indeed, it would seem to be a contradiction. Therefore, in inquiring into the natural attributes of God, we are not to expect to find any infinite effect in his works; but from the fact that he is a First Cause we find the implication irresistible that he must possess certain attributes, and that they must be infinite in degree. But I must proceed to name some of them.

II. WHAT ARE THE NATURAL ATTRIBUTES OF GOD?

1. SELF-EXISTENCE.

By this I mean that the ground of God's existence is in his own nature, and consequently that his existence is unconditioned. He exists of himself. Not that he created himself, for he never began to be; but that he has in himself the quality of necessary existence. This, it will be seen, is implied in his being the First Cause. If he is the First Cause, he is of course uncaused; if uncaused, he never began to be. If he is and always was, it is simply because he possesses this attribute of self, or necessary, existence. This attribute is then plainly implied in his being the First Cause of all finite existences.

2. IMMUTABILITY.

Immutability is another of his natural attributes. This is also implied in his being a First Cause and a self-existent Being. I have defined self-existence to be a necessary existence; a necessary existence exists necessarily; exists just as it does necessarily, and therefore must be incapable of change either from within or from without itself. Change in a necessary existence is a contradiction; that is, a necessary existence must necessarily exist either in a quiescent state, in a state of rest, or in a state of change. In whatever state it necessarily exists, therein precisely it must remain; and to say that this state can be varied is a contradiction.

3. ABSOLUTENESS.

The absolute is the unconditioned; and by this attribute we understand that God's existence is above all conditions. All finite existences are conditioned, and we cannot conceive of them as existing except under the conditions of time, space, and cause. That is, we necessarily conceive that they must exist in time and space, and have been caused. But God, the absolute, is above conditions of time and space, and sustains no such relations to them as that his existence is conditioned upon theirs. This is implied in his being a necessary existence.

4. INFINITY.

Infinity is a natural attribute of God, and a quality of all and each of his attributes. Our finite idea of infinity is that of the unbounded; and of this there are several modifications. We conceive of a mathematical line of infinite length; that is, as unlimited in length. Here we affirm infinity only in one direction. We may affirm a thing to be infinite in more than one respect or direction, without affirming infinity in the highest or absolute sense. For example, we can conceive of two lines of infinite length, but one inch apart. Now the space contained between these two lines we can affirm infinity in two respects: First, that it is infinite in length, because it has no ends; and secondly, that it is infinite in the real amount of its superficial area. But in another sense we affirm it to be finite. In two respects it has no limits; it has no ends, and consequently no whole to it in superficial area; but upon both its sides it is limited. Thus it is that in our conception of infinite, infinites may differ in real amount; as mathematicians teach us, may be multiplied *ad infinitum*.

But when we affirm infinity as an attribute of God, we mean by it that he is infinite in the absolute sense; that there is no limit to his being in any direction; no bound is set anywhere to his being; that there is no faculty of his nature that is not absolutely infinite.

120

This must be implied in his self-existence; for his existence, we have seen, is necessary; and necessary existence, we have also seen, can neither be annihilated nor changed by any conceivable power. But if God has any attribute that is not really infinite, it is conceivable that it might be changed. Indeed, it cannot be self-existent; and if it be not necessarily existent, it might be annihilated or changed. But [if] it is necessarily existent, which is implied in his being a First Cause, then it must be infinite in the highest possible sense.

5. LIBERTY.

Again, liberty is another natural attribute of God. By liberty is intended the inherent quality of self-activity, or self-action in either of two or more directions. His nature must be such that he originates his own actions, and is an entire sovereign in acting in one way or another. Liberty also implies that he acts one way or another upon occasions presented to his intelligence, and not under any law of necessity whatever. Liberty in this sense is implied in his being a First Cause. If he had been a necessary being, in the sense that he cannot abstain from acting in the precise manner in which he does act, it would follow that he must have been a Cause from eternity, which is a contradiction. If he is not free in regard to his actions any more than he is in regard to his existence, then it would involve the absurdity, as has been said, of his being an eternal Cause, and events would have been eternal; which is impossible. Liberty, then, is implied in the fact of his being a First Cause.

6. OMNISCIENCE.

Again, omniscience is a natural attribute of God. By omniscience is meant the actual and necessary knowledge of all objects, actual or possible. In other words, by omniscience is intended infinite knowledge. When omniscience is affirmed to be a natural attribute of God, it is intended that God does not obtain knowledge by study, reflection, or experience, or that he obtains knowledge at all; but that all knowledge is absolutely necessary to him. This is implied in his self-existence. Although he exists above the conditions of time and space, yet he necessarily exists in all duration, and in all space. All objects of knowledge, possible or conceivable, must, from the very nature of his existence, be known to him. That he has knowledge is implied and manifested in the universe which he has created; that he has vast knowledge is implied in the very structure and laws of the universe; but that he has infinite knowledge we know from the fact that every attribute of him, who is self-existent, must be infinite. To this it has been objected that God cannot be omniscient, or infinite in knowledge, because there are no infinite objects or knowledge, the whole creation being but finite. To this I answer, God is himself an object of infinite knowledge, and he must know himself.

7. OMNIPOTENCE.

Again, omnipotence is a natural attribute of God. I have said that cause is power in efficient action; and it has been shown that God is Cause, and the First Cause of all finite existences. That power, then, is an attribute of God, is certain, because he is a Cause. By omnipotence is intended power or ability to do whatever is an object of natural power or of infinite power. Infinite natural power cannot do what is not an object of natural power. For example, it is not an object of natural power to influence the choices of free moral agents. This is an object of moral power; that is, of persuasion, argument, and the presentation of considerations adapted to stimulate the actions of the will. The creation and government of the material universe, and the creation of the spiritual universe, are objects of natural power. Now by infinite power is intended power or ability to do whatever is an object of natural power. Natural power cannot perform contradictions. It cannot cause a thing to exist and not to exist at the same time; but it can do all things that are doable by natural power. That God is a power, or possesses this attribute, is implied, I have said, in his being a Cause. Its absolute infinity is implied in his being a First Cause; for we have seen that a First Cause must be self-existent and infinite in all its attributes.

Dr. Dwight maintained the omnipotence of God upon the ground of this affirmation, that power to originate existence, to create in distinction from to form, implies infinity; that that power which could originate any existence could self-evidently originate all existences, and could do anything that is an object of natural power. This may be true. I think it is. But nevertheless it is not true in such a sense that all minds must admit it. But I think that all minds must admit that a necessarily existent Being must be infinite in all his attributes; else his attributes might be annihilated or changed—That is, it is conceivable that they might be. But of an absolutely necessary existence we must affirm that change from that state in which it necessarily exists is impossible and a contradiction.

Power is certainly an attribute of God. As God is a First Cause, self-existent and infinite in all his attributes, he must be omnipotent in regard to all his natural attributes. I may say, that we necessarily conceive of them as unlimited. I have said in a former lecture, that we necessarily transfer our conception of ourselves to God, and conceive of him as being like ourselves, only as infinite while we are finite. We know ourselves to be causes, but limited in our power; we know God as a Cause, and irresistibly conceive of him as unlimited in his power. We cannot conceive of him as unlimited in his power. We cannot conceive of anything as impossible to God that does not involve a contradiction.

8. ETERNITY.

Again eternity is another natural attribute of God. I have said that God, the self-existent, is above the conditions of time and space. That is, time or duration, as separate from God, is not a condition of his existence. He inhabits eternity, but his existence is not conditioned upon it. By the eternity of God, then, is intended that he sustains no such relation to time or duration that he passes through it, or that his existence is measured by it, or that he grows older. Never having began to be, with him, properly and strictly speaking, there is no time, past, present, or future. All creatures exist under relations of time; their very existence passes through successive moments; they grow older; they have a constant succession in their exercises and thoughts; consequently their consciousness is constantly varying. God is omniscient; his consciousness must always be one.

I said, with him, strictly speaking, there is neither time past, present, nor future: it has been common to speak of God as filling eternity in such a way as that all time is present to him. In a certain sense this is true, but not in the sense in which time is present to us. The word present is relative, implying a past and future—that there is something else beside the present. As the word self implies not self, as the term here implies a there, so the term present implies a not present. In respects to all creatures God sees that there is a present, a past, and a future; but with him, strictly, there is neither.

We speak of time in respect to God as an eternal now. But if by now is implied a not now, if by now is to be understood as distinguishing present time from time that is not present, this is not speaking with exact propriety of God. We are finite, and our understanding conceptions cannot grasp this truth. Our understanding cannot even conceive of God as being above the conditions of time and space. Our reason affirms that if God is the absolute self-existent Being, he can sustain no such relations to time as those sustained by all finite beings. In communicating with us he speaks of himself in a manner adapted to our understanding conceptions of him. As we are confined to space he speaks of himself as being in every place, without meaning to say the he sustains any such relations to place as we do. As time past, present, and future are realities to us, he speaks of himself in a manner adapted to our practical conceptions of him. He indeed affirms that time to him is no lapse; that he "inhabits eternity;" and "that one day to him is as a thousand years, and a thousand years as one day;" meaning by this, as he must mean, that all succession of events in time as they appear and are to us, are not so to him. The end is present to him from the beginning; and therefore by the eternity of God, we mean that his existence necessarily fills all duration.

What to us is eternity, past and present, is the same to him. He fills all; but his existence is independent of duration. He fills all the duration antecedent to creation, all duration present and future to created beings; to him it is and must be a unit. Reason says it must be; for it would contradict our rational conception of God to suppose that he grows older, or that anything is otherwise to him than that we call present to us—"The same yesterday, today, and forever."

That eternity in the sense explained is an attribute of God is implied in his self-existence. He never began to be, he never can cease to be; and yet he grows no older. Much confusion has arisen by attempting to grasp the infinity of God's attributes with the understanding. Our understanding conception of God is that of a finite being, sustaining substantially the same relations to time and space that we do; that is, that he is living on from generation to generation; has come on in his existence from eternity, and passes on to eternity; and that things with him are past, present and future.

So also our understanding conception of God is that he is every-where; and yet that whereness is properly affirmable of God, and that the only difference between him and us in this respect is that his existence is indefinitely extended—this not our rational conception. I have spoken of extension as belonging to God. In the first place, it is proper to say that extension is not a quality of mind in the sense in which it is a quality of matter. Matter is a space-filling substance, is bounded on all sides, is solid, and therefore has form and dimensions, a part here and a part there. Mind is in no such sense related to place. It is not a space-filling substance; it is not surrounded by space in any such sense as to have form and limit. It is not a part of it here and a part there; it has no right or left sides. Of the actual essence of mind or matter we know nothing, except their attributes. The attributes of matter necessarily give it location in space; but the attributes of mind, thought, willing, feeling, do not locate in space—these need no place. The comprehension of this is perhaps impossible; yet we know it as a fact that no attribute of mind is dependent on the existence of space, or is so related to space as to imply that it has form or extension.

9. UBIQUITY OR OMNIPRESENCE.

This leads me ninthly to say, that ubiquity is a natural attribute of God. Ubiquity is omnipresence. From what has just been said, it will be inferred that by this I do not mean that whereness is properly predicable of God, and yet we cannot speak of him without supposing him as somewhere. It is true that he is in all space, yet his existence does not occupy or fill space in the sense of excluding anything from it, nor in such a sense that its existence is a condition of his existence. Space is the condition of the existence of body, but not of mind.

That God exists, we have seen; and that he exists of necessity, and therefore every attribute of God must be infinite. Now in the sense in which it can be truly said that God is anywhere, it must be said that he is everywhere; understanding that by whereness we do not mean to predicate locality of him. I have said that he cannot with respect to his own existence say, I am here, or anything is here, for here implies a not here, or there; and there is not there, or not here, in respect to God's existence. In regard to finite beings, he sees that there must be a here and a there, and up and down, a this way and a that way, a this side and a that side; but in respect to his own existence, there can be no such thing; and such words convey no meaning when applied to the real existence of God. All is alike here to him; and yet not here in any sense that implies that we predicate whereness of God otherwise than as affirming that there is no limit in any direction to his existence, that wherever space is he is, and all of his nature and attributes are alike omnipresent. His is not extended in the sense that a part of him is here and a part there, but all his attributes are in every place.

10. SPIRITUALITY.

Again, spirituality is a natural attribute of God. When we speak of matter or of spirit, we do not mean to be understood as knowing the substratum of any existence, material or spiritual, except as we know it in and through its attributes. Matter is known to us by the perception of certain attributes; mind or spirit is known to us by the conscious exercise of natural attributes. We irresistibly affirm that attributes inhere in substance; that substance is and its attributes are. By spirit we mean that substance that thinks, wills, feels. These attributes have nothing in common with the attributes of that which we call matter. Matter is space-filling, spirit is not space-filling; matter has form, spirit has not; matter has solidity, matter has inertia, spirit is active; matter is extended in the sense of part here and part there, spirit is not extended in this sense.

I said, spirituality is an attribute of God. Our necessary conception of God is that he is Spirit, as we are spirit. Not that he has a material body, as we are aware of having; but that he has a spirit without body. His spirituality is implied in his self-existence, and in all his natural attributes—immutability, absoluteness, liberty, omniscience, omnipotence. Indeed it is impossible, if God were material, that he should be infinite, that he should be a first cause or self-existent. If material and self-existent he would be under a law of inherent necessity. If he were material, as matter is made up of particles, he could not be infinite; for an infinite number of particles is an absurdity. If he were material, or space-filling, he must exclude the existence of all other material substances. For if material and omnipresent, he must be infinitely solid, or the spaces would not be filled with God. He could not be solid and infinite, but yet porous. Indeed it is impossible to conceive of God as an infinite material existence; but as a first, free, self-active, Cause, he must be Spirit.

11. MORAL AGENCY.

Again, moral agency must be a natural attribute of God. I have said that we naturally conceive of God as possessing a nature like our own, A moral agent is one possessing intelligence—including conscience or moral intelligence, sensibility, and free will. We ourselves are moral agents; God is our creator. We cannot conceive of God as not a moral agent. I said, a moral agent is one possessing intelligence—including conscience, sensibility, and free will. I should have added to this—existing under conditions of intellectual development; that is, possessing actual knowledge. There is a distinction to be taken between a moral being and a moral agent. A moral being is a being possessing the attributes above named. An infant before reason is at all developed is a moral being; a man in sleep is a moral being; a man in a fit of insanity is a moral being; but in none of these cases is he a moral agent.

Moral agency implies the possession of these faculties and the natural exercise of them; that conscience should exist as a faculty and be in a state of development; and that the moral being should be awake, and rational as opposed to insane. In other words, the moral being must exist under conditions of the present knowledge of duty, in order to be a moral agent. We necessarily affirm of God that he is good, morally good; and in this assumption is implied our necessary conviction that he is a moral agent. If not a moral agent he cannot have the ideas of right and wrong; he cannot be under moral law; he cannot have moral character. But all men do necessarily conceive of him as having moral character; this is our *à priori* conviction or necessary assumption.

We have seen also that through the medium of conscience we know God as Moral Governor: this implies that we know him as a moral agent under the relation of Supreme Ruler. But again, moral agency is implied in God's being a first cause. That he has created moral agents is proof conclusive that he has the idea of a moral agent; and his being a first cause shows that he is free. Now if he knows what a moral agent is, and is free, he must have the powers of a moral agent; and being free and omniscient he must in fact be a moral agent. Again, if God has reason, conscience, sensibility, and free will, he must be a moral agent. He must act and act morally, or under moral responsibility to his conscience. He does not necessarily act right, for this were a contradiction. But he must act right or wrong. He must be a moral actor. This is the true idea of a moral agent.

12. UNITY.

Unity is a natural attribute of God. By this is intended that God is not made up of parts in the sense of particles; or in the sense of possessing various members, as bodies have members; or in the sense of being more than one substance. This is implied in his infinity; in every sense in which he is infinite he must be a unit—I mean, so far as his existence is concerned. This infinite essence or substance may posses many capacities or qualities, and be capable of doing, feeling, thinking, infinitely; nevertheless as substance it is one and identical, and cannot be composed of finite parts; for no number of finites could make an infinite, nor even approach the infinite in the least degree. In his essence he must be one; in his capacities he may be many.

13. INDEPENDENCE.

Independence is also a natural attribute of God. By independence is meant that he exists independently of all other existences; and in the exercise of his attributes is entirely independent. This is implied in his self-existence, and in his being a First Cause. By independence I do not mean that God can deny himself, that he is independent of the subjective laws of his own existence, that his will is independent of his moral nature or conscience; but that in his being and in the exercise of his attributes he is a law to himself. This is implied in his self-existence and infinity.

14. NATURAL PERFECTION.

Natural perfection is one of his attributes. That is, his nature is absolutely perfect; no conceivable improvement could be made in it. This is also implied in his self-existence. Our necessary conception of God is that of a being infinite in all his attributes; no conceivable improvement could be made in them; in other words, the conception of any limit to any one of them is impossible.

LECTURE X.

THE MORAL ATTRIBUTES OF GOD.

I. WHAT IS MORAL CHARACTER, AND WHAT ARE MORAL ATTRIBUTES?

1. THE moral character of a being must reside in his voluntary actions. This is the unequivocal testimony of conscience. It is impossible for us to conceive that moral character should reside in involuntary acts, which are unavoidable.

2. Again, I remark, that moral character must reside primarily, not in a refusal to choose, for that is no choice, but in the ultimate choice of a moral agent. By ultimate choice I mean the choice of an object for its own sake. Every moral agent, from the necessity of his nature, chooses either to please God or to please himself, as his ultimate end, that is, for God's sake or for his own sake. Either God's interest must be practically regarded by him as supreme, and he must choose that as the supreme object of choice; or he must be selfish. In other words, he must either be benevolent, love God supremely and his neighbor as himself; or love himself supremely. The good of God and his universal kingdom is of infinite value in itself. Every moral agent is bound to choose this for its own sake; and this is good-willing or benevolence.

Opposed to this is willing self-gratification; a practical treating of self as if the gratification of our own desires, appetites, etc., were of supreme importance. Now in this ultimate choice of the good of universal being, or of self-gratification as an ultimate end, moral character must reside. Primarily, surely, it can reside nowhere else. It is this ultimate choice that gives direction and character to all the subordinate actions of the will; that gives direction to the volitions, the actions, and the omissions of all our voluntary lives. This ultimate choice is the root or fountain from which all volition and all moral action spring.

I say, moral character resides in this ultimate choice, and is as this ultimate choice is. If this choice is that of the highest good of universal being, supreme love to God and [love] to our neighbor equal to our love of self, it is benevolence, and the very essence of virtue or righteousness. If this choice be that of self-gratification, this is selfishness and sin, and the very essence of moral evil. Observe, then, benevolence is willing the natural good of universal being. It is willing that state of mind that constitutes and is implied in the highest blessedness of which any being is capable. This choice is moral good or virtue. Moral good, then, or virtue, consists in the choice of natural good, or the blessedness of being for its own sake; while sin consists in choosing to gratify our own desires to the neglect of other and higher interests that do not belong to self. Benevolence, then, is the impartial choice of the universal good of being; sin is the choice of self-gratification and not good of all in the desire of the intrinsically valuable to being.

3. Again, a moral attribute must be a permanent quality of this ultimate choice. Moral attributes are not like the natural attributes, qualities of the essence or substance of a being; they are the qualities of his ultimate choice or intention. If he is benevolent his moral attributes are moral qualities of his benevolence; if he is selfish, they are the moral qualities of his selfishness.

Benevolence being an ultimate choice, a standing committal of the mind to the good of universal being, certain qualities inhere in it as implied in willing the highest good of God and the universe. So with selfish ultimate choice; it is the committal of the will to one's own personal gratification as its supreme end, and in this certain qualities inhere and are implied. These qualities of benevolence on the one hand or of selfishness on the other, are the moral attributes of the benevolent or the selfish being. These qualities being elements or qualities of benevolence or selfishness, will manifest themselves in volitions and corresponding actions as their occasions arise to call forth the expression of them. Thus they reveal themselves; but this we shall see in its place.

II. GOD IS MORALLY AND INFINITELY GOOD.

1. This no moral agent can doubt. Every moral agent, from the very fact that he is a moral agent, affirms his obligation to love, obey, and trust in God implicitly and universally. Hence, every moral agent by a necessity of his nature does assume that God is

infinitely good; and although his dealings may be entirely mysterious, totally inexplicable, and so far as we can see, unreasonable, yet the conscience will affirm his infinite rectitude, and hold us responsible for obedience and submission under all circumstances. This shows that the goodness of God is a first truth of the moral reason. It is a truth that everybody knows; a truth necessarily and universally affirmed by every moral agent. When I say that it is a first truth of the moral reason, I do not mean that God is necessarily good, for a necessary goodness is a contradiction; but I mean that he is infinitely good, and that all moral agents know it and affirm it. Indeed, more than this may be said; moral agents know that he cannot be God if he were not infinitely good; that if he is to be regarded and treated as God, the Moral Governor, exercising rightful authority over the whole universe, he must be infinitely good. And here let me say, that we have no means, properly speaking, of proving the goodness of God, just because it needs no proof.

But, then, there is another reason. God is infinite and we are finite; we can grasp but a very small portion of his ways. Now it is true that we can find in the world around us very many indications—indeed, indications innumerable—of the goodness of God; but then there are so many things inexplicable, that if we were left to judge merely from facts that occur under his providence, we could not arrive at the logical conclusion that he is perfectly and infinitely good. Nor could we arrive at an opposite conclusion. The facts, so far as they can be known to us, would utterly baffle all efforts on our part to arrive at a settled conclusion. For, as we shall see, many of his moral attributes are but very partially revealed as yet in his providence, and we shall also be able to see why this is so.

Again, God is infinite, we are finite. He cannot make to us an infinite revelation, just because we could not understand it. He cannot make us understand his far-reaching plans, and his reasons for what he does. Many of his dealings are therefore to us necessarily mysterious, and not infrequently appear unreasonable and unjust. The goodness, I have said, of a being resides in his ultimate intention. Now while it is manifest in innumerable instances that God is kind and good, yet there is so much in the complications and seeming inconsistencies of the vast machinery of the universe, that we of course are not able to take in this ocean of mystery, and from it logically prove that God is infinitely wise and good. Nevertheless, we have a certainty that this is so, surpassing that of mere logical demonstration. We are so constituted as to irresistibly know that God is infinitely wise and good. We know that he is a moral agent; we know that his moral character must be either infinitely good or infinitely evil. The assertion that God is a wicked being is revolting to the human mind, and we cannot possibly receive it. No moral agent can entertain with any honesty the conception that God is otherwise than infinitely good. I said, the universal and necessary conviction that we ought universally to obey him, implies that he is infinitely wise and good, and that we know it.

2. The goodness of God must consist in unselfish love or benevolence. The universe, so far as we can search it out, is a unit in the sense that all its parts are so adjusted as to be under one universal law; that is, the material universe as we know it is governed by the universal law of gravity, all the parts being bound together in one system.

Again, all moral agents, we know, are under one law; not the law of necessary action, like the material universe, but the moral law, the law of free action; or in other words, they are under the law of liberty in the sense that they are left to choose in accordance with this law or in opposition to it, and abide the consequences. When I say they are left free to choose, I mean that the actions of their will are not necessitated; they are under moral obligations to choose in accordance with this law, but are not necessitated to do it. They have power to choose or refuse; but they must abide the consequences. Now in looking into the material universe, so far as the principles of science can go, we see that the one set of material laws is so adjusted as to promote the well being of all sentient existence in just so far as these laws are obeyed. There seems to be contrivance and design in the whole framework of material nature. Our bodies are "fearfully and wonderfully made;" and a consideration of every part exhibits the most striking evidence of the benevolence of the Creator. Volumes have been written on this subject; and were all written that might be written upon this interesting question, we might say with John, that "the world could not contain the books that should be written."

3. But again, the moral law, or the law for the government of moral agents—not that to which they do universally conform, but that to which they ought universally to conform—requires perfect and universal benevolence. This is a direct revelation of God's will in respect to his creatures.

4. Again, God is a moral agent; and we know also that this must be his rule of action. Being a moral agent he has a conscience; and his conscience must postulate as his rule of action this same law of universal benevolence. Thus he is a law to himself: his virtue consists in obeying this law.

He made us in his own image and wrote this law in our very nature; that is, he has given us a conscience that irresistibly and irreversibly postulates this same law as obligatory upon us. Thus he has revealed his own benevolence in the very construction of our nature. He has so made us that we affirm our universal obligation to be benevolent; and also we affirm universally that he is benevolent. Now, if God is not benevolent he does not deserve the respect of the subjects of his government, and has no right to govern. But we cannot possibly conceive ourselves as not under obligation to obey him upon the assumed knowledge that he is perfectly and universally benevolent and not selfish.

I said, that we could not prove by an examination of facts that God is benevolent. By this of course I intended the outward facts of the universe. But when we consult our irresistible convictions and the law of universal benevolence which he has impressed as our rule of duty upon our very nature, we learn with intuitive certainty that God is benevolent. We do not, therefore, need to go abroad to interpret the whole of his vast creation, we do not need to have a history of all God's doings and an explanation of them all to give us reasonable satisfaction that he is benevolent; we know it *à priori*; we know it in the irresistible convictions of our own minds, and in the law of benevolence which he has so impressed upon our nature that it is impossible that we should not impose it upon ourselves.

This law of benevolence we know to be subjective in the sense that every subject of it, that is, every moral agent, affirms it to be his own rule of duty. And every moral agent also affirms that this law is objective as well as subjective; that God imposes it on him and requires obedience to it. When moral agents affirm obligation to be benevolent, they affirm this obligation in the name of God. They always and necessarily conceive themselves as amendable to him.

III. TWO OBJECTIONS THAT HAVE BEEN MADE TO THE BENEVOLENCE OF GOD.

1. The existence of so much misery in the world. To this I answer:

(1) That God could not have chosen this misery for its own sake. He is a moral agent; and it is impossible that a moral agent should choose misery for its own sake. For this would imply the choice of it universally, and hence the choice of his own misery for its own sake. But this, as we have said, is abhorrent to the very nature of a moral agent; misery cannot be to a moral agent an object of choice for its own sake.

(2) But again, this misery God could not have chosen as a means of gratifying himself; that is, he cannot be a malevolent being in the sense that he ever desires misery for any delight he can take in it on its own account. Misery considered by itself and in its own nature is abhorrent alike to the will and the sensibility of every moral agent.

(3) Again, this misery that exists in the universe was not the end God had in view in creation, for misery is not a good but an evil; and we have seen that we necessarily conceive of God as benevolent. This necessary conception of the benevolence of God forces us to the conclusion that misery was no part of his end, that it was not chosen for its own sake. Nevertheless it exists: now the existence of this misery is not inconsistent with the benevolence of God; it must, therefore, be incidental to the best possible universe that he could make.

In strictness we are not called upon to reply to this objection, unless he who urges it can show that the fact of the existence of so much misery under the government of God is utterly inconsistent with his benevolence. This he cannot show. He cannot show that this misery is not disciplinary in this world; and he cannot show that any degree of misery that may exist in the future world will not conduce to the highest good of the universe as a whole. We are not bound then to show how the existence of misery can be reconciled with the benevolence of God. The burden of proof is on the objector, to prove that it cannot be consistent with the benevolence of God. We have shown by the most conclusive evidence that God is benevolent; but here he brings up certain inexplicable facts, and would insist that these facts are inconsistent with the positive proof that God is benevolent. But this he must prove, and this he cannot do. Even the misery that is in the universe may all be overruled as a means of the highest ultimate good. The contrary cannot be shown; but until it is shown, the objection is good for nothing in the presence of the positive proof of God's benevolence of which we have spoken.

2. Secondly, the existence of moral evil, or sin, has been urged as a proof that God is not benevolent. But in answer to this objection, I observe:

(1) Sin is voluntary, and consists in selfish acts of free moral agents. God, therefore, cannot be the author of sin; for the sin being a free, voluntary act, can have no author but the sinner himself. The freedom of the will is essential to moral government and moral obligation—God has made men free moral agents, in his own image; and he regards this freedom of will as sacred. Now, it cannot be shown, in the first place, that it was possible under a moral government to exclude all disobedience; but until this is shown, the objection is good for nothing. "But," says the objector, "Christians assert that God is infinitely powerful, and wise, and good. Now if he is infinitely wise he must have known, when he created moral agents, that they would sin if he did not interpose to prevent it; if he is infinitely powerful, he certainly might have prevented it; if he is infinitely good, he certainly would have prevented it."

But how does this follow? To be sure his omniscience does imply that he knew that if he created moral agents, they would sin unless he prevented it. Now it is supposable that in view of this he might have declined creating them; or, after he had created them, that he should have interposed and so ordered the administration of his affairs as either to abridge their liberty of will, or shut them out from temptation, or have annihilated them and thus prevented their sin. But observe, if he had never created moral agents and established moral government, there could have been no virtuous creature in the universe. Again, if he had adopted such measures, and so created men that they had been less free and had less temptation, then their virtue would not have been so valuable as it now is.

Again, it cannot be shown that any possible administration of a strictly moral government could wholly have prevented sin; or, if any possible administration could have prevented sin, that upon the whole such administration would have resulted in greater virtue and happiness than the one now adopted. It may be that the wisest system naturally possible even to omnipotence, has been adopted. It may be that both sin and misery are unavoidably incidental to a perfect moral administration; and therefore, that they could not have been wisely prevented; that to have so changed the whole order of arrangement as to have prevented both sin and misery, would have been, upon the whole, so benevolent and wise an arrangement as the one now existing. I said this may be: it can never be shown that the present system is not the wisest and best possible system. The burden of proof is on the objector. But he cannot prove this; and until he does his objection is invalid.

But we may take stronger ground than this: we may say that by the very laws of our nature we are forced to the assumption that the present system, with its incidental evils, is the best possible. This is implied in God's being infinitely wise and good; and this we know he is. He requires of us by his unalterable law to will and do the most good that we can; he requires of himself the same. He cannot have preferred a less to a greater good, a less perfect to a more perfect system. The system that is must be the best that can be, or God is not infinitely wise and good. It cannot be shown that it is not the best that can be. Our irresistible convictions affirm that with all the mystery involved in it to shortsighted creatures like ourselves, yet the system is as perfect as infinite attributes could make it; and that it will result in the greatest good that infinite power and goodness can secure.

These two great objections, then, the existence of natural and moral evil; amount to nothing in the face of all the positive proof of God's benevolence. It is admitted the they involve a world of mystery to our shortsightedness; nevertheless, we know that God is good, infinitely wise and benevolent; and that all this that is so mysterious to us is clear to him, and that which he can see to be consistent with his infinite perfections. And here it is worthy of remark, that the benevolence of God appears strikingly in this, that he has so created moral agents that they shall necessarily assume his goodness. From the nature of creatures who begin to be they must begin to learn; and much that is mysterious must necessarily be involved in the vast plans and government of God. These things cannot be explained to creatures who are, as we are, in the infancy of our being, because we are in no position to understand the explanation. God sees the end from the beginning. We see not a step before us; all the future is entirely dark, so far as our knowledge goes. But then we are forced to assume and cannot but affirm that "God is light, and in him is no darkness at all;" that although "clouds and darkness are round about him, yet justice and judgment are the habitation of his throne;" that in the midst of all this, so mysterious and trying to us, we can still say with certainty that God is right, that this is all consistent with his infinite benevolence, and will be fully explained when we are able to understand the explanation. In the meantime, we fall back upon our irresistible convictions, that God has never done or suffered anything that was not consistent with infinite benevolence.

IV. WHAT ARE THE MORAL ATTRIBUTES OF GOD?

Having shown sufficiently that God is benevolent, we now proceed to inquire respecting the qualities or attributes of this benevolence. I have said that an attribute of benevolence is a permanent quality of it; by which I mean that such is the nature of benevolence that it is disposed to do, and not to do, certain things.

The attributes of benevolence are of course all voluntary, that is, they are permanent qualities of a voluntary state, or of ultimate choice. Again, many of them are indicated in the works, and providence, and grace of God, as manifested in this world; but they are more specially known as being implied in the nature of benevolence, a goodwill to the universe, and especially goodwill to moral agents. It is especially by inquiring what must be implied in disinterested benevolence, that we learn what are and what must be the moral attributes of God.

1. JUSTICE.

Justice must be a permanent quality of God's benevolence. Justice is that quality of benevolence that disposes it never to wrong any being, but to treat all beings according to their intrinsic desert, that is, according to their moral character. This must be a quality of benevolence. The manifestation of it consists in rewarding the righteous and in punishing the wicked. But it is a quality of benevolence, and benevolence is goodwill. Now God will manifest this quality of his benevolence in regarding the righteous universally; but it does not follow that it will be manifested where the general good of the universe can dispense with the infliction; for observe, benevolence seeks the highest good of the universal being. The attribute of justice will never allow of any injustice; no being who deserves reward can fail of reward. But, as I have said, it does not follow that benevolence will always execute penal sanctions and take the forfeiture at the hand of one who deserves punishment, where the general good may be secured and yet the infliction dispensed with. For God is not only just but merciful; and it must be remembered that all his moral attributes are attributes of benevolence, and therefore that they will be so manifested as best to secure the highest good of universal being.

But of this attribute it should be further said, that in this state of being it is not to be expected that it will be universally manifested in treating moral agents just as they deserve. This is certainly a state of probation; it is therefore out of place to administer retribution here. Here we are to expect that the justice of God will wait until probation is finished before it is executed by the infliction of penal sanctions. Indeed, it were impossible that in this state of existence, God should deal with every moral agent as he sees that they deserve. Knowing as little as we do of the motives of men, it would perhaps be impossible for mankind to believe that God was administering impartial justice, should he deal with men precisely according to their character as it appears to him. It is at the close of probation, when a grand assize has been held, and all the facts in the history of every individual made known, that this attribute of justice is to appear in exercise. In the providence of God, there is just enough here and there of an expression of his regard to rectitude to awaken attention and keep the conviction alive that God is just; while there is so much in his providential dealings that came short of justice as to leave the fact on the face of his providence that this is not a state of rewards and punishments.

In conclusion, then, let me say of this attribute, that we do and must irresistibly affirm that benevolence to moral agents implies a disposition to do justly. Especially must this be true in one who sustains the relation of Moral Governor, whose business it is to execute law and treat men according to their deserts. But to avoid all misunderstanding, let me say again, that the attribute of justice must forever prevent God's requiring more than is just, or failing to give to virtue its due; while in the case of forfeiture and crime, benevolence may prefer the exercise of mercy rather than to punish and execute justice, where the public good can be as well secured.

2. MERCY

This leads me to say that mercy is another of the moral attributes of God. This attribute consists in that quality of benevolence that disposes it to pardon crime, to dispense with the execution of the penalty of moral law, where the general interests of the government will admit it. It is the opposite of justice, in this: justice is the quality that disposes to execute law; mercy is the quality that disposes to dispense with the execution of penalties where it can be done without injury to the public. Justice is that quality of benevolence that disposes to treat persons as they deserve; mercy is that quality of benevolence that disposes God to deal with sinners better than they deserve, and even the opposite of that which they deserve. Justice disposes to reward with good where good is deserved; mercy disposes to confer good where evil is deserved. These must both be attributes of benevolence; and whether the one or the other shall be manifested in any given case, must depend upon whether the highest good can be secured by the manifestation of one or the other.

That mercy is an attribute of God, we have said, must be from the very nature of benevolence; but the existence of this attribute is plainly indicated in the forbearance exercised towards sinners in this world. Men are in fact sinners. But they are not executed. God is sparing them, and thus expressing his goodwill toward them. Instead of treating them justly, or inflicting upon them unmitigated evil, as they deserve, he is bestowing on them innumerable blessings. This is fact. Now from this it might be reasonably inferred that he is disposed to do them all the good he wisely can, notwithstanding their crimes; and that if it be possibly consistent with the public good he will pardon their crimes, and not take the forfeiture at their hands.

But again, I remark, it is very plain that mercy cannot be exercised under a moral government except upon two conditions: The first is that the sanctity, dignity, and authority of moral law shall be sustained. That is, that the law shall not be dishonored, first, by the sinner himself in disobeying it; and secondly, by God, in lightly setting aside the execution of the penalty without exacting anything that shall assert the authority and sustain the honor of the law. In other words, public justice must be sacred; that must be done which will as thoroughly sustain the authority of the law as the execution of its penalty would do, or the exercise of mercy can never be admitted. The law requires benevolence, that the highest good of being shall always be consulted and secured in the administration of the government of God. This law is to remain the eternal law of God's government. If it be dishonored by sin, the public good manifestly requires that its authority shall be reasserted by requiring a sacrifice of such a character as shall effectually sustain its authority, effectually declare God's indignation against sin, his love of holiness, his determination to sustain his law, and that shall as effectually rebuke sin as the execution of the penalty would do.

The law is public property, it is God's rule of action as well as ours, imposed on him by his own nature as it is imposed on us by our nature. He cannot repeal or alter it. He may do whatever benevolence may do; and this is consistent with his law. If the law be disobeyed, he must execute its penalty, or some substitute must be provided of a nature that will be understood by his creatures to restore the honor of the law. This must be done as a condition of the exercise of mercy. Were this the place, it might be shown that to meet this necessity was the design and end of the atonement of our Lord Jesus Christ. But I pass to say, that a second condition upon which this attribute of mercy can be exercised is the entire reformation of the sinner himself. I say, the entire reformation. Sin is voluntary; and while he continues in sin he cannot be forgiven. It is totally inconsistent with the administration of law to pardon the transgressor while he persists in transgression.

Benevolence must delight in the exercise of mercy from its very nature. It is goodwill—delights to do good and to confer good. It delights to bless, and has no pleasure in a curse for its own sake.

LECTURE XI.

THE MORAL ATTRIBUTES OF GOD
(CONTINUED).

3. VERACITY.

VERACITY is that quality of the divine benevolence that disposes God to keep faith with his subjects. His veracity is the condition of our obligation to believe him. But how shall we prove the veracity of God? If God is at all veracious, he is perfectly and infinitely so. Truth has been defined to be the reality of things; and truthfulness, or veracity, a disposition to represent things as they are. It is plain that conformity to truth must be essential to the highest well-being of moral agents; and it is a universal conviction in the minds of all moral agents that veracity is a duty, and that conformity to truth is essential to the highest well-being of the universe.

We cannot prove the veracity of God by any external evidence; our knowledge of his ways is too limited to enable us to prove it from the facts of creation and providence known to us. Nevertheless we are sure that veracity is a quality of the divine benevolence. All men are certain of this; and this accounts for the fact that no man questions whether God is to be believed, if it is settled that he has spoken. The question is not, Is God to be believed? But, Has he spoken? and What has he said? The fact settled that God has spoken, and the interpretation agreed upon of what he has spoken, and all men consent by irresistible conviction to our obligation to believe him. His affirming his own veracity in the Bible would not to us be conclusive evidence that he is veracious, had we not the revelation of this in our own nature. He has so created us that we approve of veracity and abhor a liar. No man, however wicked, can approve of lying, or respect a liar. All men necessarily disrespect a liar; and all men would irresistibly disrespect God if they thought him a liar. But no man does, or can suspect God of lying. He has fastened the conviction of his veracity upon us by a necessary law of our being; it would shock us as blasphemy were God accused of lying. Therefore we do not need external proof of the veracity of God; for we have within us a proof that puts the question beyond all doubt. Our own nature proclaims it, and asserts it with an emphasis too strong and deep to be resisted.

It should be remembered that veracity is an attribute of benevolence. It expresses and reveals itself in keeping faith with his creatures for their good, and for the public good; its ultimate end always being the promotion of the highest good of being. The promises of God are of no value except upon the condition that veracity is one of his moral attributes. We trust his promises no farther than we have confidence in him in this respect. If we do not regard him as veracious—if it be not settled with us, not merely as a conviction, but if our will be not committed to this conviction and in the attitude of trusting him, that is of confiding in his veracity, his promises will not avail us. If we plead them, we shall not rest in them. Hence it is that his promises are so little used. Many there are whose hearts are not in sympathy with his veracity; whose hearts are not committed to this attribute of love. They do not confide in it; hence to them the promises are of no avail.

4. DISINTERESTEDNESS.

By this is intended unselfishness. When the disinterestedness of God is spoken of, it is not intended that he is not interested in his creatures; but rather that he is interested in them, but not for selfish reasons. He loves them with unselfish love; his goodwill to them is really goodwill to them. He seeks their good for their own sakes. He wills their well-being from an unselfish interest in them. But here the inquiry arises, how shall we know that unselfishness, or disinterestedness is a quality of the divine benevolence. I answer, first, it enters into the very conception of benevolence. Benevolence is good-willing, that is, willing the real good of being. On this the choice terminates. It is not the willing of the good of another for the sake of our own good; but it is making good an ultimate—that is, the good of being; and it is from regard to the being whose good we will. Therefore, it is in its own nature unselfish; it is chosen as an ultimate, and not because of its relation to ourselves. Good to self is not the end, but good to the being or beings whose good we will. But it should be said, that disinterested benevolence does not imply that we have no regard whatever to our own good. The command as it lies revealed in the conscience is, "Love thy neighbor as thyself." Not, love thy neighbor and hate thyself; but love thy neighbor as thyself. Our own good is of as much value as the good of our neighbor; and the promotion of our own interest is as important—that is, may be as important—as the promotion of the good of any other. Furthermore, the securing of our own good is committed particularly to us; and we are held responsible for the securing of our own good.

But the way to secure this is by unselfishness; by laying no undue stress at all upon our own interest, and in regarding the interests of others in ever instance according to their relative value. This same law is God's rule of conduct. Disinterested benevolence in him does not imply that he has in his willing no regard to his own good. This were infinite folly, and even wickedness in him. His is the supreme and infinite good. The aggregate of the good of all creatures cannot be brought into comparison with his; for his is infinite, and the good of all others is only finite, and therefore as nothing in comparison with his. Of course, God ought to love himself supremely, or to be supremely benevolent to himself. To will the good of others rather than his own would be to will the finite instead of the infinite; to reverse the true order of things, and prefer an infinitely less to an infinitely greater good in his regards. Disinterested benevolence, then, in God, must necessarily lay supreme stress upon his own good, because it is infinite.

So, when he requires his creatures to love him supremely, he only imposes the same law upon them that he does upon himself in this regard. All men knowing that God's is the supreme good, are certain that they ought to be supremely benevolent to him. That he may be blessed supremely, infinitely blessed, is what all men ought to wish with all their hearts. This is a universal conviction of moral agents, that they ought to love God supremely, to choose his pleasure rather than their own, to prefer his interest to their own and the interests of all other beings, and supremely to devote ourselves to the doing of his pleasure.

By Charles G. Finney.

Let it be understood, then, that by disinterestedness in God, we mean that quality of his benevolence that disposes him to will the good of his creatures from regard to them; to lay just that stress upon their good which by its intrinsic importance renders reasonable. He has no selfish reason for promoting their good, but does it for their sake. And this is indeed the only possible way in which he could promote his own good. Were he selfish in his goodwill to others, this could not meet the demands of his own conscience and could not therefore result in his blessedness. It could be no real satisfaction to him to will the good of others selfishly, because the very selfishness of the willing would render it impossible for him to enjoy it. To will their good disinterestedly, for their sake, and promote their happiness rather than his own, is that which gives him enjoyment in this exercise, being conscious that he is disinterestedly willing their good for its own sake. He enjoys the good which he confers upon them. He seeks their will-being because he is interested in it; therefore when he promotes it and secures it, he is completely satisfied; he has that which he sought. He was interested in them; he sought to do them good for their sakes; and when he sees that he has secured that which he sought he is happy, and enjoys the good which he has conferred even better than they do. Hence Christ says, "It is more blessed to give than to receive." Thus it is that disinterested benevolence secures his own good in seeking the good of others. He promotes his own highest glory and happiness in disinterested devotion to the good and happiness of others. Just so it is with benevolence in all beings. This is the divine economy of disinterested benevolence. Every disinterestedly benevolent being promotes his own true happiness and interest best by unselfishly devoting himself to promoting the happiness of others; and thus while benevolence denies self, it therein and thereby promotes the good of self in the highest possible manner.

But how do we know, I inquire again, that this is a quality of the divine benevolence? This question I answered before by saying that disinterestedness enters into the very idea of benevolence. But now I observe, that we are so constituted as irresistibly to know that God is not selfish but benevolent, and that unselfishness is a

146

quality of his benevolence. It is irresistibly affirmed by us, that God is good, perfectly and infinitely good; that unselfishness is essential to moral goodness, and that selfishness is sin; therefore all moral agents necessarily know and assume the unselfishness of God; and there is no such thing as really convincing them that he is selfish. We need not go into the outward universe, and into the history of his providence, to prove that he is unselfish. So little do we know of what he has done, and is doing, and will do in the universe, that historically we may not be able to demonstrate that he is unselfish; but he has not left himself without a witness in nature. This conviction is necessary and universal, and no moral agent can doubt it; and this is the end of all questioning upon the subject. To be sure the facts of the universe known to us strongly indicate the unselfishness of God; but to all these it might be answered, that we know not the ultimate end which God may have in view. All these arrangements for our happiness and well-being may be only such arrangements as slave-holders make for the health and comfort of their slaves; or as men make for their domestic animals, having self in view in all they do. They pamper their pets, and feed their slaves, and do all that they do with the design at last to promote their own interest and pleasure. Now it might be said, as it has been said, that the fitting up of this world so comfortably, and even so beautifully, might be consistent with a selfish ultimate design; so that skeptics may cavil in regard to the ultimate or perfect benevolence of God. But to put this beyond all question as a matter of conviction, God has given us a conscience which irresistibly assumes his unselfishness; so that we cannot persuade ourselves, nor can the devil persuade us, that God is selfish. We know irresistibly that he is not.

I further remark upon this subject, that questions like this can only be conclusively settled with us in the way in which they are settled [?]. Our finiteness, our limited knowledge render it impossible for us to know enough of the ways of God, historically to settle the question beyond all doubt that he is unselfish. Therefore this question might be left in agonizing doubt, even in the minds of the highest order of finite intelligences, were it not revealed to them as an irresistible and certain conviction. It is an *à priori* intuition, or revelation of the fact of God's disinterestedness in the laws of their own being. This is satisfactory; this lays a broad foundation for the repose of faith. This is that which his creatures need; being unable to grasp and understand by an examination of his ways the whole history of his doings, they need a firm foundation upon which to rest. His government over moral agents is moral. The condition of sustaining it is implicit confidence in him; and this confidence in creatures needs a firmer basis of conviction than could be laid by what they can now, or do know historically, of his ways.

Many of his dispensations are not only involved in the greatest mystery, but are often exceedingly trying to us, and no doubt to all his creatures. He cannot give any such high policy of his government, and thus settle us upon the broad basis of historical facts; hence he has so created us that from the earliest moments of our moral agency, we affirm his disinterested benevolence, and that unselfishness or disinterestedness is a quality of his goodness. We assume this as a condition of affirming obligation to obey him. If we could doubt the one, we should deny the other.

5. FORBEARANCE.

Forbearance is that quality of the divine benevolence that disposes him to bear with the infirmities and even sins of his subjects. When they oppose him, trample on his authority, he is not hasty to take the forfeiture at their hands and punish them according to their deserts; but is slow to anger, waits, gives them time to consider, and bears long with their abuses. We are so created that we could not call a being perfectly or infinitely good who had not the attribute of forbearance. Of this attribute we can say that we have the evidence in our own experience that God is forbearing. It is also a matter of observation. We can gather multitudes of evidence in the facts around us of the forbearance of God. We know from our own consciousness that he has borne long with us; we see that he does the same with others; and here we have the evidence both of consciousness and sense that forbearance is one of the moral attributes of God. We also have this attribute given as an irresistible conviction. As we regard God as infinitely good, as infinitely and disinterestedly benevolent, we know that he will not be hasty and impatient, but will forbear as long as he wisely can.

This follows irresistibly from the fact of his unselfish benevolence, and is implied in it. This attribute is manifested in this world in a most striking manner. Its manifestation lies upon the very face of his dealings with ourselves and with all the world around us. Nay, the very existence of our sinful race is only a demonstration of the existence of this attribute, and an instance of its manifestation. Reflecting minds are often greatly affected by the manifestation of this attribute. It is truly marvelous that God should forbear to execute his wrath upon the rebellious and most provoking race of men. No fact is more visible on the face of the world than the forbearance of God as manifested to men.

6. LONG-SUFFERING.

By this is intended that quality of his benevolence that suffers himself to be abused, disobeyed, dishonored, for a long time, without executing vengeance. This attribute is also most strikingly manifested in our own history, and in the history of our race. No one surely can doubt that this is an attribute of the benevolence of God. Nay, he has often exercised it to such an extent as greatly to try the faith of some of his servants. He has borne and suffered so long as that, for a time, it was a temptation to them; and they have inquired whether there was a righteous God that ruled the universe. The seventy third Psalm affords a striking illustration of the trial which God's friends are sometimes subjected to by the exercise of his long-suffering.

7. SELF-DENIAL.

Self-denial is that quality of benevolence that disposes us to deny ourselves some good for the sake of promoting a higher good of others; to forego some enjoyment or volunteer some suffering of our own as a means or condition of warding off the sufferings of others, and securing to them a greater good. It is manifest that this must be an attribute of disinterested benevolence. Disinterested benevolence is the willing of the good of being for its own sake; consequently it implies the laying the greatest stress upon the greatest good. It does not will good to self because it belongs to self, but the good of being for the sake of being in general. The highest practicable good is that which benevolence seeks; consequently it lays the greatest stress upon the greatest good. From its own nature, therefore, it will forego a less good to self for the sake of a greater good to others. It will volunteer to suffer a less evil for the sake of warding off a greater evil from others. It seeks to secure the highest good that can be secured to whomsoever it may belong.

Self-denial, therefore, for the good of others, when a greater good can thereby be obtained, is necessarily a quality of disinterested benevolence. This attribute of God is greatly manifested in this world. It was this attribute which was peculiarly manifested in the atonement of Christ. "God was manifest in the flesh;" gave his Son a voluntary substitute to suffer and die for guilty men. This was no doubt the most illustrious exhibition of self-denial ever seen in this world, and perhaps in the universe. Self-denial by no means implies selfishness, but always the reverse. True self-denial is the opposite of self-indulgence. It should be remarked that true self-denial is not inconsistent with the highest happiness of God or any other being. It is an attribute of benevolence; and if a benevolent being volunteers to prevent the greater suffering of another, or forego any particular form of good to self for the sake of promoting the higher good of others, this is by no means to deprive himself of any real ultimate good.

Nay, such self-denial as this really affords greater enjoyment than the refusal, under circumstances where it is demanded, could possibly yield. Nay, true self-denial is the only condition of enjoyment in a moral agent where it is demanded by the great law of benevolence. In the exercises of self-denial, if it be true and genuine, we are necessarily satisfied with ourselves. This is the condition of our highest personal enjoyment. Our enjoyment is not that at which we aim; for this would be no self-denial. The aim is to promote the good of others by denying ourselves. Benevolence is really sincere in making the sacrifice with a single eye for the sake of the end, that is, the greater good of others. Their good is the end; we give up a certain good of our own, or volunteer a certain suffering of our own, with the simple disinterested intent to promote their good. Now it is just because we are thus disinterested in this self-denial, because self-denial is real, intelligent, and genuine, that it produces satisfaction; and thus by reaction upon ourselves gives us even more satisfaction than is obtained by those for whom we deny ourselves. Thus it is that in the atonement of Christ, although the sacrifice on the part of God was real and great, nevertheless it must have been a source of infinite satisfaction to him; and hence it is said of Christ, that "for the joy that was set before him he endured the cross, despising the shame." He also declared that it was more blessed to give than to receive. The self-denial of God, then, must be a condition of his happiness, as it is the condition of his self-respect, the condition of his being infinitely and perfectly good.

But, let it be remembered, that self-denial in him, as in all other beings, is unselfish, as I have said. It was his love to the world, to sinners themselves, that led him to give his only begotten Son to redeem them. Christ laid down his life for our sakes; with the intention to bless us. From unselfish regard to us, he "endured the cross and despised the shame." Nevertheless, with the knowledge that it would promote his own happiness just in proportion as with a single eye he aimed to promote our happiness; just in proportion as he sought not his own interest, he secured it; just in proportion as he denied himself, he secured that at which he did not aim, to wit, his own highest honor and eternal satisfaction.

But how do we know that self-denial is an attribute of the divine benevolence? Suppose a skeptic who denies the atonement should ask how we know that God will deny himself. Skeptics often evince their great ignorance by the low and even blasphemous thoughts they entertain of God. They will often represent God as being infinitely too high to notice creatures so small as we are. They think it ridiculous to suppose that God would give his Son to die for such a race as that of man. They think it infinitely below his dignity to deny himself for our sakes. But this shows their vast ignorance, and how little they have thought of what is implied in the infinite goodness of God. It was not beneath the infinite dignity and divine greatness to create us, surely it is not beneath his dignity and greatness to care for us. Indeed, in this is his true greatness most strikingly manifested, that he cares and expresses his regard not only for the greater, but for the least of all his creatures. He stoops to number even the hairs of our heads; and not a sparrow can fall to the ground without his notice and commiseration. Who, after all, could call him supremely and infinitely good if he were unwilling to take pains to secure the eternal well-being of creatures whom he had made? Who could after all say that he met their whole ideal of moral perfection in its infinite extent, if he would refuse to volunteer even a suffering, and a great suffering, to save even his guilty and inexcusable enemies from eternal suffering? Who could say that their whole ideal of moral perfection was met by a being who would not stoop to the capacities, and miseries, and sufferings, and circumstances of every creature of his hand, to do them good? And especially where this self-denial must so commend itself to his own nature as really to conduce to his happiness at last, and ultimately to deprive him of no good; or in other words, where from the very nature of God and of self-denial, the exercise of self-denial would be really a source of blessedness to him? Indeed, this is the true idea of moral goodness, it finds its own blessedness in doing good.

To real perfect goodness, personal suffering to relieve others is a luxury. Self-denial for the promotion of the greater good of others is essential to securing the great end upon which the will has fastened; it is the only possible means of meeting our ideal of what we ought to be, and of securing that upon which our heart is set. Our very conception, then, of infinite goodness, is that self-denial must be an attribute of it. Such is our necessary conception of unselfish benevolence that this quality must belong to it; it must be disposed to forego a less good to self for the sake of the higher good of others. And this, I say again, is true economy; for the higher good in this case is in fact obtained, and obtained too without any ultimate loss to the individual sufferer, or the one who denies himself. From the very laws of his being, his sufferings and his self-denial will react and be a luxury to himself.

8. IMPARTIALITY.

Impartiality as a moral attribute does not imply that all beings, whether virtuous or vicious, are to be treated alike, for this would be partiality. It would not be the treating of persons according to right reason; it would be making unreasonable discriminations; or rather demands. Impartiality is that quality of benevolence that disposes it to make no unreasonable discriminations; to treat all persons and all interests as the highest good of universal being demands; never showing any favoritism that is unreasonable or inconsistent with the law of right or benevolence.

I have said that it would be partiality, and impartiality, to treat the righteous and the wicked alike in their ultimate destiny. The present is a state of probation, not of rewards and punishments. Here moral beings may be treated as not having finished their probation; hence God causes his sun to rise upon the evil and upon the good, and sends rain upon the just and upon the unjust. This attribute of God, from the very nature of a state of probation, is not uniformly manifested to us in this world. Indeed, so ignorant are we that to us it often seems that providential discriminations are unequal and partial. But they only seem to be so. It can never be shown that God is impartial in any of the discriminations which he providentially makes, or in the bestowment of his grace. The fact that one is rich and another poor, that one is born in this and another in another country, one in this age and another in that, one in the enjoyment of certain privileges of which others are denied; the fact that some have the Gospel and others have not—the facts around us are innumerable of both gracious and providential discriminations, the reasons of which are by no means always apparent to us. Nevertheless, it cannot be shown that God has not benevolent reasons for every one of these discriminations. If he has benevolent reasons, and is therefore obliged by the very law of benevolence thus to discriminate, if upon the whole he sees that these discriminations are wise and demanded by the highest good of being in general, then he is not partial but impartial. It can never, therefore, be shown that God is partial.

But how shall it be shown that he is impartial? I answer, first, it is implied in the fact of his infinite goodness and his unselfish benevolence. If he is infinitely wise and good, as we know he is, it is impossible for him, remaining good, to be otherwise than impartial in the sense already explained. He has benevolent reasons, and must have, for all the discriminations he makes in his treatment of his creatures; and this is impartiality; this we know intuitively to be a quality of unselfish benevolence.

Men are disposed to complain of God as if he were partial; and yet they know he is not. It is true that his dealings are often trying to our shortsightedness and ignorance, and especially to selfishness; but he has not left himself without a witness. We have within, if we will but reflect upon it, the irresistible conviction that God must have infinitely good reasons for all the discriminations which he makes, and for all his dealings with his creatures; that although, in this respect, clouds and darkness are round about him, yet impartial justice and judgment are the habitation of his throne.

9. BENEFICENCE.

Again, by beneficence is intended that quality of the divine benevolence that disposes God to great liberality and bountifulness in the bestowment of favors. In other words, it is that quality of his infinite benevolence that disposes him to exert his infinite attributes for the promotion of the well-being of his creatures. Benevolence is ultimate choice, is good-willing; beneficence is that quality that disposes to the carrying out of good-willing in the life and action in the promotion of that good upon which the ultimate choice terminates. This quality of the divine benevolence is very strikingly manifested in his works and providence. The whole creation in its laws and order and arrangement, are only so many manifestations of the beneficence of God.

10. SOVEREIGNTY.

By sovereignty is intended that quality of his benevolence that disposes him to act in accordance with his own discretion. He has nobody wiser than himself to consult, and takes no counsel of creatures in regard to the best way of serving the highest good. He, therefore, in creation, providence, and grace, bestows his favors in a manner that meets his own views of propriety and fitness. He never does injustice to anyone; he never omits any act of kindness or opportunity to do good to any of his creatures, where in his own judgment it would be wise and conducive to the highest general good for him to interpose. But he consults his own discretion. How else could he do? And the sovereignty of God is nothing else than infinite love directed by infinite wisdom.

Sovereignty is no arbitrary exercise of power on the part of God. It is not the doing of his own pleasure capriciously, or a disposition to do this or that way in a capricious manner; but it is simply that quality of his benevolence that disposes him to act in his own wisdom, in accordance with his own view of what is best to be done and most conducive to the highest good. If God were not sovereign in this sense, he would not be worthy of respect. It is no doubt his duty to exercise entire sovereignty in this respect in all his dealings with his creatures, never doing them an injustice, but bestowing favors according to his own discretion. And who can fail to see that such a sovereignty is worthy of God, and that the contrary would be infinitely unworthy of him? Who has a right even to desire that he should do other than exercise this sovereignty and act in accordance with his good pleasure?

It cannot be too distinctly borne in mind that God's attributes, natural and moral, are and must be revealed to our irresistible convictions by an *à priori* intuition, as the condition of our affirming our universal obligation to obey them and submit under all circumstances. To prove to ourselves or to others *à posteriori* the existence of these attributes in God, would require an amount of study and knowledge that few possess. God has not left us to the necessity of all this study before we affirm our obligation to obey and trust him, but has so constituted us that we necessarily affirm from the earliest development of reason, the existence and perfection of all his attributes. If we were really in doubt respecting the attributes of God, we should necessarily be in doubt regarding our obligation to obey, trust, and submit. But this we never can be.

LECTURE XII.

THE MORAL ATTRIBUTES OF GOD
(CONTINUED).

11. FIRMNESS.

FIRMNESS is that quality of the benevolence of God that disposes him to abide by that which he sees to be wise and good at all events. The love of God seems to be regarded by some as what we call mere good nature. It is spoken of as if it were an emotion of fondness, a state of mind that paid comparatively little regard to moral discriminations and distinctions, or to moral principle; a disposition to gratify all classes; and a kind of tenderness that cannot endure to be severe and firm in the execution of law, even though severity and firmness be demanded by the public good. We are sometimes asked, Would a parent execute such wrath upon his children? Could a parent punish forever? And thus the love of God is supposed to be parental really in the sense of parental weakness; but it is perfectly apparent on the face of the universe that God's love is not a weakness, as that of parents often is. Who does not perceive on the face of the world's history a succession of events that show that God is anything but weak, and yielding, and undiscriminating in his love and dealings with his creatures?

Skeptics have stumbled at the Bible because of its representations of the severity with which God deals with his creatures. There is an aspect of inflexibility, firmness, and even sternness, sometimes presented in the Bible representations of God, from which they turn away. They seem disposed to represent God as all mercy. Indeed, it is plain that they so understand his love to consist in a disposition rather to pet and indulge sinners, than in a disposition thoroughly to administer a moral government for the public good. But how strikingly is the firmness of God manifested in the administration of physical government, and in the history of earthquakes, of pestilences, or shipwrecks, of storms. If physical law is violated the chariot of his providence is driven axle-deep

156

through the blood and bones of those who have thus thrown themselves before it in the violation of the laws of the material universe. What earthly parent has firmness enough to see a ship freighted with his own children dash upon the rocks, or go to the bottom in a storm! What earthly parent could endure to see among his own offspring, or even among human beings anywhere, what God is witnessing every day and every hour! And these desolations only evince his inflexible firmness in the execution of the laws of his providential government. Skeptics who reject the Bible because of its representations of the inflexibility and severity of God, would do well to take lessons of him in the administration of his physical government. They confounded the parental with the governmental relation.

It is perfectly plain that it is the same God who rules in the material universe, that has revealed himself in the Bible. His love is not a weakness. It can endure the trial of doing what is necessary to be done to sustain his government, cost what it may. It required great firmness to support his own authority by sending his Son to make an atonement for sin. It required great firmness to destroy the cities of Sodom and Gomorrah, to destroy Jerusalem, to destroy the old world with a flood; but his love is equal to it. It is not cruelty in a ruler to sustain wholesome laws and order, and secure the public good, if need be, by severe measures. It is an infirmity and a weakness in a ruler when he cannot endure to take the measures that are essential to the public weal.

From the very nature of God's benevolence and omniscience, it must be true that he will not yield a point where the public good demands action. He is a ruler; he cannot consult private feelings at the public expense. His compassion is great; his forbearance is great; he delighteth in mercy and judgment is his strange work; yet his firmness is equal to the trial of executing vengeance and carrying out the measures necessary to secure the good upon which his heart is set at any cost.

12. SEVERITY.

This term is used sometimes in a bad, and sometimes in a good sense. When in a bad sense it implies selfishness, when in a good sense it is an attribute of benevolence. As applied to God, severity is that quality of his benevolence that causes him to take stringent but benevolent measures in promoting the public good, where these are needed. We often see occurrences around us that to us appear to be severe. They are, however, never so in a bad sense. They are only strong and decided measures demanded by the exigencies of his moral government. It should be remembered that God's benevolence is a righteous benevolence, a holy, sacred benevolence, a sin-hating benevolence, a law-sustaining benevolence. Severity, then, in a good sense, must be one of its attributes. There is a point beyond which forbearance is no virtue in a ruler; these are occasions on which hesitance and holding back the bolt of justice were ruin.

What striking instances we sometimes see in providence. A little neglect on the part of a mother, a little ignorance or indiscretion in the nursing of her child, and the result is that it expires in agony in her arms. A slight carelessness and a habitation is burned with all its inmates. A ship is sunk freighted with missionaries, or with multitudes of souls in no way implicated in the carelessness. Nevertheless, they had committed themselves to the conduct, superintendence and providence of the captain and the crew, and they must abide the consequences. No words can adequately describe the apparent severity of some of the dispensations of providence. Now these are facts in the universe of God; and they are quite as difficult to reconcile with our ideas of benevolence and goodness as any recorded in the Bible. Why, then, should the Bible be rejected, and yet the existence and government of God in the universe be admitted?

Cases have occurred in which the radically orthodox views have been rejected because of the severe aspect in which they represent the character of God. But logical necessity forced the same persons to reject the Bible for the same reason; and then to reject the providence of God for the same reason; and ultimately of course to reject the very existence of God. Facts are facts. The world is; these facts are; God is; God is love; these facts are consistent with his love. They are accounted for only by the fact that his love is disinterested benevolence; a law-promulgating, law-sustaining, just, holy, as well as merciful love. It is often necessary for a parent to exercise wholesome severity, a benevolent severity, in the treatment of his children. It is often so with rulers of states and nations; it must be so in every government; and a good ruler must have firmness, and sometimes must exercise severity.

Severity does not imply injustice, does not imply cruelty, but the reverse. It were unjust to the public not to execute laws, and to deal sternly and severely when laws are set at naught and efforts made to upturn the foundations of society and government, and destroy all good. Sometimes Universalists appeal to the prejudices and selfishness of men by inquiring, Would you banish one of your children forever? Would you be so cruel as that? What earthly parent would do it? And do you represent God as worse than human beings? I answer, No; but he is infinitely better. Earthly parents are too weak and often too wicked to take the needed measures to control their children, even for their own good. But suppose a parent to have a large family of children, and suppose his oldest son to be exceedingly profligate, and to set himself deliberately to debauch and ruin the morals of the whole family. He persuaded the younger sons to drunkenness, the daughters to indelicacy and uncleanness, and the whole of them to rebellion against parental authority. Suppose that no entreaty or influence that the parent can use can restrain this son. Now it is no want of benevolence in the parent to banish this son from his house. It were cruelty to retain him; if he cannot be restrained he must be banished. The father has no right to indulge his parental feelings toward him to the injury and ruin of all the rest of his children. How absurd to appeal to him and ask, Are you so cruel as to banish this son from your house forever? It is more pertinent to ask, Are you so cruel as to allow this son to ruin the whole family?

Just so it is under the government of God. His government is moral, not physical and a government of force. It is a government of moral law, moral considerations and persuasions. Now if moral considerations will not restrain, then sinners must be destroyed. It is cruelty to the universe at large to let them go unpunished, when all appropriate means have been used for their reformation. In such a case, longer forbearance were a crime and not a virtue. Love that would not punish is a weakness and an infirmity, and not that which becomes a ruler.

13. EFFICIENCY.

Efficiency is that quality of the divine benevolence that disposes God to be active, energetic, and zealous in the promotion of the great interests of the universe. God's love, remember, is benevolence and not an emotion. Emotions may have no efficiency; and the same is true of passive affections and feelings of fondness. They may expend themselves in feelings, in tears, or smiles, or petting; but such is not the nature of God's love. It is the infinite will in a state of committal to the public good. It is infinite energy; and it is the energizing of this love that hung out the heavens, created the entire universe, and that rolls the wheels of his government, both natural and moral, with an almighty power and energy.

The benevolence of God is an ultimate choice, or committal to the promotion of good. The attribute of efficiency gives existence to the executive volitions that create and govern. The volitions of God that appear in time, that create, sustain, and govern the entire universe, are nothing but expressions of the efficiency of his benevolence. He is spoken of in Scripture as being clothed with zeal in the execution of his purposes as with a cloak; and when great and wonderful things have been predicated, it is said that the zeal of the Lord of Hosts will do this.

By efficiency, then, as an attribute of the divine benevolence I mean, that it is the quality of his benevolence to be infinitely active and persevering in the accomplishment of his great designs. He does not say, Be ye warmed and clothed, and make no efforts; he does not pity, and exhaust himself in feeling that produces no good; but his executive volitions flash with infinite power over the entire universe; and the forked lightings are only the faintest glimmerings and expressions of the infinite energy with which he pursues his course.

14. SIMPLICITY.

Simplicity is the quality of unity. There is no mixture in the benevolence of God. He is said to be love. He has but one end to which he is devoted; thus ultimate choice and purpose are a unit, always one, always the same.

All the forms of virtue of which we speak resolve themselves, in their last analysis, into qualities or attributes of benevolence, as we have seen in these lectures on the moral attributes of God. Virtue, then is one. It consists in benevolence; and its various expressions and manifestations are but expressions and manifestations of one state of mind, to wit, goodwill. That God's benevolence is un-mixed, we know by an irresistible conviction. We cannot conceive of God as being otherwise than perfect.

15. IMMUTABILITY.

Immutability is one of the moral attributes. Choice is conditioned upon some object of choice. When the will has made its election and committed itself, it cannot change its position except upon the condition of some motive, or at least apparent reason for doing so; or perhaps it is more correct to say, that the will receives all the considerations and influences which are conditions of its action, either through the intellect or the sensibility. When the will has chosen, either the intellectual views must be changed, or the feelings must be changed, as a condition of the will's changing; otherwise the will would change its purpose, choice, or preference, without any conceivable or possible object. Now while it is true that no feeling, no desire, no thought, no intellectual discovery or consideration can force the will; yet some feeling, desire, thought, or intellectual apprehension or consi-deration is a condition of choice. In other words, the will's actions are conditioned upon some consideration presented through the sensibility or intellect as an inducement to choose. If it be a feeling, the will may act to gratify it; if it be a thought or intellectual perception, an object then is presented as a reason for its action. All creatures are finite. The intellectual perceptions and the feelings of finite beings are subject to continual change; so that immutability can be no attribute of their goodness or of their sinfulness. But it is not so with God. God, as we have seen and shall soon farther observe, is infinite in all his natural attributes and in all his moral perfections. He is naturally omniscient; and no new thought or intellectual view can ever be present as a condition of his change of choice. Being omniscient, all the considerations that make him feel are eternally present necessarily considered, and are seen with all the force with which they ever can be seen. Hence, there is infinite fullness, stability, and immutability in all his feelings. His consciousness is one.

Now, if God be absolutely infinite, his mind has from eternity been made up, and that too in view of every possible or conceivable consideration presented either through his intelligence or his sensibility, that can be conditions of his change of mind. Now as his whole being is a unit and present, his whole experience and consciousness an infinite and present fullness, change with him is a contradiction. Nor is this inconsistent with his eternal goodness. If in view of every conceivable reason for choice, he has chosen once for all, and his choice is forever immutable, his virtue is all the greater for that. He has committed himself without any variableness or shadow of turning, with a certain knowledge that he never should change, and with a solemn intention never to change.

Now to speak after the manner of men and say, that his continuing in this state is no virtue if change is impossible to him, is absurd. For the only reason why change is impossible to him is because every conceivable reason for action has been taken into the account, and his mind unalterably settled. The stability, therefore, and immutability of his goodness is one of its infinite excellencies, for the reason that it actually embraces and acts in accordance with every possible consideration that ought to influence mind.

But strictly and properly speaking, God does not live on as we do through successive periods of his own existence without change. Change in us is change in consciousness. We are aware of change only by the changes in our consciousness. Did not our consciousness change we should have no conception of the passage of time. Time to us would be only present, did our consciousness always remain the same. But for changes in consciousness, time past, present, and future would have no signification. It should be

162

understood that the absolute omniscience of God renders it certain that his consciousness is invariable. The conception is of course beyond our comprehension, as the infinity of all his attributes is. We know that so it must be, but when we attempt to grasp it, it must be true, it is higher than heaven; we cannot attain unto it. We know it must be true, and yet we cannot conceive how it can be true.

Should it be asked, since God is a moral agent and therefore free, is not change possible to him? I answer, that the freedom of the will does not imply power to change a choice without any possible or conceivable object or reason for choice, existing either in the feelings or in the intellect. Choice is preference. The choice of a single object is preferring its existence to its non-existence. The choice of one of many things is the preference of that one to others. Choice being preference always implies comparison; the existence of a thing is compared with its non-existence, or one thing is compared with another. Now, the will's action is always conditioned upon there being some reason for preference, or change of will. And this reason may be an impulse of the sensibility, or a thought in the intellect. But where no objects are brought into comparison; where the existence of one object cannot be compared with its non-existence; where the intellectual views cannot by possibility change, as in the case of absolute omniscience; where feelings cannot by possibility change, as is also the case with absolute omniscience—in such cases freedom of will does not imply power to change when the will is committed in view of all the considerations possible or conceivable that might be the conditions of change.

I have spoken of the immutability of God as consisting in the impossibility of change. This inability to change is found in this, that there can be no conceivable reason for change. The most capricious being cannot change his choice except upon the condition of some change of thought or feeling. So that the certainty that God will not change is owing to the fact that he is committed with infinite strength and there is no conceivable or possible reason ever existing in the intellect or sensibility that can be conditions of change. Strictly speaking, God is immutably good because he fills eternity and has no time to change.

16. INFINITY.

By infinity is intended that there is absolutely no limit to his benevolence. It is not partial, it is universal; it is not merely to finite creatures but to himself as the infinite; it is goodwill to universal being; it is eternal; it is the choice of his whole mind; it is the devotion of all his attributes, by the act of his will, to this end. It is therefore an ocean, having neither shore nor bound; it is as illimitable as his nature. We know that infinity, immutability, and all theses attributes, must be attributes of the divine benevolence, because he is infinite. We intuitively affirm that as his natural attributes are infinite, so his moral attributes must be infinite.

17. HOLINESS.

The last attribute that I shall name is holiness. Holiness is that quality of benevolence which is often represented as moral purity; the infinite opposite of all blemish, impropriety, or inconsistency. Holiness is sometimes spoken of as if it comprised the whole character of God; and it must be a quality of all and each of his other attributes. It seems to me that, strictly speaking, it is the quality of symmetry or harmony in his attributes; that quality that adjusts them to each other. For example, God's character is that of perfect moral excellence. We are so constituted that we could not recognize a character as perfect that was all justice or all mercy, all forbearance or all severity, all meekness or all firmness. Indeed, all these qualities of benevolence must be adjusted one to the other; and there must be a law of adjustment, of harmony, of proportion and symmetry pervading the whole of them, else the character would be out of balance. There would be a want; it could not to us realize our ideal of moral beauty and perfection. Should we see a man who was all justice and sternness, we might call him a just man, but should not conceive of him as a perfect character, as a holy man. Should we see a man all compassion, we should feel that he was not a perfect man. Were he all meekness, or all mercy—or take any one of the moral attributes of goodness, it would make a moral monster rather than a symmetrical goodness. We conceive of that character as holy that is symmetrical; and we can conceive of no other character as perfect in holiness except that of symmetry.

Some writer has compared holiness in character to the law of harmony in music. Musical sounds to make harmony need to be adjusted to the subjective laws of harmony that belong to our nature. These sounds must sustain certain relations to each other to be agreeable to us, and to make harmony. Throw them out of this relation, and they produce discord, dissonance, and not harmony. But when these relations are perfect in respect to their distances, and their volume and quality of sound, then the harmony is perfect; our ideal of perfect music is realized, and there is nothing left to desire. So in regard to moral character; there must be harmony; there must be a law of adjustment, proportion, and symmetry in all the moral elements or attributes that make up the character. These must be adjusted to our subjective ideal of perfect goodness. When this symmetry is seen, when this perfect adjustment of moral perfections stands revealed to the mind, our ideal of moral perfection and beauty is realized; and there is no greater joy than results from standing in the presence of unlimited holiness. In the descriptions of heaven in the Bible, it is remarkable that it is the holiness of God that excites their enthusiasm, that inspires their awe, that inspires their praises; and the cry of "Holy, holy, holy," while they veil their faces, thunders throughout the upper sanctuary.

But how do we know that God is holy? I reply, we cannot conceive of God as being other than infinite in moral goodness, and we cannot conceive of infinite moral goodness as of God as other than infinitely holy. We therefore, by the very laws of our nature, irresistibly assume the holiness of God. Our consciences ever recognize him as the perfection of moral purity; hence we are shocked at the suspicion of his being otherwise than perfectly and infinitely holy. We revolt at the conception, and cannot for a moment admit the possibility.

REMARKS.

The foregoing are some of the moral attributes of God. These qualities of benevolence are most of them indicated either in his moral or providential government. They are clearly revealed to us in our irresistible convictions of what he must be. The progress of his kingdom will no doubt reveal to his creatures many moral attributes or qualities of his benevolence never yet suggested to finite beings. Neither his justice nor his mercy, as they are now understood, may have been so much as thought of in their appropriate signification, until the occasion of their manifestation existed in the universe. So in the progress of his dispensations occasions may arise that may develop in the thought of his intelligences qualities inherent in his benevolence never yet suggested to the mind of a finite being. Of this we may rest assure, that nothing can ever occur in the eternity to come that shall not find in the benevolence of God some quality that will cause it to meet the emergency, and adapt the dispensations to the occasions.

Thus there are many forms of beauty, yet undeveloped in action, before the minds of creatures; and there may be no end absolutely in the eternal future to the new and striking revelation of the moral attributes of God. In these consist his true glory. When Moses prayed, "Show me thy glory," he passes by and proclaimed the name of the Lord, and suggested to Moses several of his moral attributes as constituting his peculiar glory: "The Lord, the Lord God, gracious and merciful, long-suffering, abundant in goodness and truth, keeping mercy for thousands, forgiving iniquity, transgression, and sin, and that will by no means clear the guilty." Exod. 34:6.

From this short view taken of the natural and moral attributes of God, it is clear that his eternity and infinity are devoted to the promotion of the highest possible good. As he requires us to do, so he does. If he requires us to will and do good, he wills and does good himself. He leads the way in every virtue by his own example. And what inconceivable results are yet to be seen by the universe of creatures! What an infinite privilege to be under such a government! To have such a Father, possessing infinite natural attributes, with a heart unalterable to wield them for the highest good of his creatures, and the highest interests of the whole universe!

Again, it is plain that the government of the entire universe is safe in his hands. Nothing can surprise, nothing can defeat him. He

166

will do all his pleasure, in the sense that he will accomplish all the good that he has proposed to himself, and will not be defeated. There is ground of infinite security for the righteous, and of infinite terror on the part of the ungodly who persist in wickedness.

The study of theology is the study of God and his attributes; of his laws, dealings, providential arrangements—indeed, all truth that can be known to us is but a part of theological truth, or truth respecting God and his affairs, either moral or material. A theological student will make but little progress unless he views everything in a theological light. All truth is symmetrical; all truth emanates from our common center; its relations, proportions, and beauty cannot be seen out of adjustment with the system of truth.

Our finite capacities cannot take in the whole field of truth in its symmetrical adjustment; and yet it will be the study of ages upon ages to all eternity. Its unity, simplicity, symmetry, will be more and more felt, as it is more and more perceived by the progress we shall make in study to all eternity. God the infinite and perfect, the First Cause, the Supreme Ruler, the great natural and spiritual Center of all being, is the object of our study. Every truth has a sacredness about it, every question a solemnity and meaning; every line of theological instruction has an importance and a sacredness to awe, and stimulate, and sanctify.

THE ASA MAHAN PROJECT.

BY ALETHEA IN HEART MINISTRIES.

THE LIFE AND WORKS OF ASA MAHAN (1799-1889).

Volume

Numerous additional articles and literary notices in the following published periodicals:

OE   The Oberlin Evangelist, 1839-1862
OQR The Oberlin Quarterly Review, 1845-1848
BH   Banner of Holiness, 1872-1883
DL   Divine Life and International Expositor of Scriptural Holiness, 1877-1889

Reproduction of the complete published writings in hard and soft covers, with detailed indexes. To be available in print individually and in a complete series; as well as on CD with full searching capabilities; also recorded on tapes, CDs, and DVDs. Each sermon and lecture to be made available as individual booklets. Mahan's contributions to *The Oberlin Evangelist, Oberlin Quarterly Review, Banner of Holiness*, and *Divine Life* included in this.

Work books and multimedia helps to be created to assist in the private or classroom study of these volumes. A presentation of the influence of Mahan upon the church and world to be given through the *American Reformation Project*.

www.ingramcontent.com/pod-product-compliance
Lightning Source LLC
Chambersburg PA
CBHW030527100426
42813CB00001B/173